AHEAD OF HER TIME

SELECT WRITINGS OF DORA RUSSELL

EDITED BY

Elizabeth Miller

Foreword by Bernice Morgan

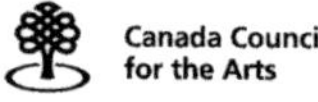

We gratefully acknowledge the financial support of the Canada Council for the Arts, the Government of Canada through the Canada Book Fund (CBF), and the Government of Newfoundland and Labrador through the Department of Tourism, Culture and Recreation for our publishing program.

Cover Design by Todd Manning • Layout by Joanne Snook-Hann
Printed on acid-free paper

Published by
CREATIVE PUBLISHERS
an imprint of CREATIVE BOOK PUBLISHING
a Transcontinental Inc. associated company
P.O. Box 8660, Stn. A
St. John's, Newfoundland and Labrador A1B 3T7

Printed in Canada

Library and Archives Canada Cataloguing in Publication

Russell, Dora, 1912-
[Works. Selections]
Ahead of her time : select writings of Dora Russell / Dora Russell ; edited by Elizabeth Miller.

ISBN 978-1-77103-068-7 (paperback)

MIX
Paper from responsible sources
FSC® C011825

I. Miller, Elizabeth Russell, editor II. Title.

PS8585.U766A6 2015 C818'.5408 C2015-904828-1

AHEAD OF HER TIME

SELECT WRITINGS OF DORA RUSSELL

EDITED BY
Elizabeth Miller

Foreword by Bernice Morgan

St. John's, Newfoundland and Labrador, 2015

To my siblings,
Rhona, June, Peggy and Kelly

TABLE OF CONTENTS

FOREWORD

The saying "a woman's name should only appear in print when she marries and when she dies," was still very much accepted in St. John's during the 1930s and 40s. This dictum rested, I presume, on the assumption that only criminal activity could result in a female getting her name in a newspaper on any other occasion. Today, with journalists such as Pam Frampton and Lana Payne writing regular thought provoking columns for *The Telegram*, it is hard to imagine a time when the opinions of women were excluded from the local press - yet that was the case. Any child growing up in St. John's when I did would have been hard pressed to name one woman who had contributed to the history or culture of Newfoundland.

Enter Dora Russell, who, in 1945 finessed her way into becoming editor of the women's page for *The Evening Telegram*, forerunner of today's *Telegram*. This was an era that condoned tokenism, when most 'Women's Pages' contained only household hints, recipes and advice to the lovelorn. It is to the credit of both Dora Russell and her publisher that *The Telegram*'s first women's editor was given the freedom to set a standard that journalists, both male and female, can aspire to.

As this volume attests, Dora Russell's interest ranged from the tourist trade to music education, from poverty to astronomy, from the content of soap operas to the problem of drunken drivers. However, in her writing for *The Telegram*, and later for *The Daily News*, the constant thread was for the engagement of women in public life.

Having advocated, to no avail, for women to be included as delegates to the National Convention, Dora Russell attended every session. Fortunately she had the ability to turn the dreariness of convention proceedings into amusing copy: "Would forty-five women have taken a week to make up their minds whether they wanted a delegation to proceed to Ottawa now or later? It did not matter a row of beans that thirty other men had said exactly the same thing. Every voice had to be raised, not once but in many cases twice or thrice."

At other times she was cutting, and deadly serious. Her 'In Defence of Reporters' is as up to date as today's news and many of the problems she pinpointed: the lack of affordable housing, the absence of women on city council, our ignorance of the wishes of people in Labrador are, sadly, still unaddressed.

I never met Dora Russell, who by all accounts was a charming, attractive and supportive wife and mother. Nevertheless, I suspect Newfoundland's first woman editor was, at heart, a subversive. She certainly used her talent and humour to reveal and undermine the deeply embedded, male dominated society of her day. Dora Russell was a woman ahead or her time - she was in many respects also ahead of our time.

Bernice Morgan
2015

INTRODUCTION

Few readers today will ever have heard of Dora Russell (1912-1986), let alone have read any of her work. Those who knew her would likely remember her as the wife of Ted Russell, renegade politician, author of the CBC radio series of the 1950s, "The Chronicles of Uncle Mose" and creator of Pigeon Inlet, the quintessential Newfoundland outport. Dora, however, was much more than just the woman behind the man.

Ethel Dora Oake was born on March 7, 1912 at Change Islands in Notre Dame Bay, the third of four children. Her parents were Jesse and Laura (Brinson) Oake. The family moved to St. John's while Dora was a small child. During their early years in the city, the Oakes lived first on Casey Street, then on LeMarchant Road and later on Queen's Road where Jesse established a grocery business on nearby Gower Street. Dora, along with her two sisters, attended Bishop Spencer College. Little is known about her school years except a few snippets provided by her friend Sylvia Wigh in an interview published in the early 1960s. As a pupil at BSC, Dora had a keen interest in both the Girl Guides and astronomy. She combined the two interests by selecting Astronomy as one of the badges she would work towards in her Guide program. Her reason for choosing astronomy? Because she knew nothing about it. For years she kept a scrapbook, clipping everything she could find out about the topic.

By 1932, when she turned twenty, Dora had moved into the public sphere. The Literary Society (a women's group) held a debate: "Resolved that women should engage in a business or professional career." We today can hardly fathom that there was a time when such a statement was even remotely debatable! A brief report in a local newspaper included this statement: "In spite of the fact that woman is supposed to be inferior to man in mental ability and stability, the affirmative was awarded a unanimous decision."

Around the same time, she wrote a letter to the editor of *The Evening Telegram* passionately objecting to the cutting of teachers' salaries, declaring such action as "a discredit to the Government, and a drastic violation of all the rules of honour and fair play."

In 1933, having attended two sessions at the Normal School for teacher training, she accepted a teaching position at St. Mary's Church of England School on the Southside. The principal, Josephine Colley, specifically wanted Dora and her friend Sylvia Wigh. In her "Reminiscences," Dora notes, "She had never had teachers capable of producing concerts. Sylvia and I had a flair for these things and made a good team even creating some ballet dances as well as the usual skits, drills, etc." Dora was also quite musical, and taught private piano lessons from her home.

While at the office of the Superintendent of Education in the summer of 1933, to finalize her first teaching assignment, Dora met her future husband, Ted Russell. They were married on January 6, 1935. Dora had no long dress to wear, and there was no reception. These were hard times. Just over a year earlier, Newfoundland - on the verge of bankruptcy - had voluntarily relinquished self-government as the legislature essentially voted itself out of existence. In 1934, the Commission of Government, comprising a governor and six commissioners appointed by the Crown, assumed power. This was to last until 1949.

In 1935, having accepted a position as magistrate with the Commission of Government, Ted set off for Springdale, his first assignment. Dora had mixed feelings about the move. Initially, she could hardly wait. In many ways, however, she was disillusioned as there were numerous adjustments, some difficult, that she as a city dweller had to make. "Some of the local attitudes," she recorded later, "were stifling. Dancing was not tolerated, nor card playing." Furthermore, the standard of housekeeping in Springdale was very high; one had to live up to it if one was to maintain the respect of others. Fortunately for Dora, maids were not hard to find, and over the years the Russells had several "servant girls." Two children were born to the Russells during the years at Springdale: my older sister Rhona in 1936, and myself in 1939. In each case, Dora felt obliged to go to St. John's for the birth.

In 1939, Dora and her family were on the move again, as Ted was transferred to Harbour Breton. Their stay would be for scarcely a year; not long enough, according to Dora, "to put our roots down." They lived in the old Newman house with a magnificent view of the bay. Dora loved it. Although she had established some very close and lasting friendships in Springdale, she found Harbour Breton in many respects a refreshing change, far removed from the taboos of Springdale. "It was good to get up a concert again and to plan dances," she recollects in her "Reminiscences."

In the fall of 1940, with winter approaching, the Russells were faced with yet another transfer – to Woody

Point, Bonne Bay. "When we arrived in Bonne Bay, not only did we have a baby practically dying of pneumonia, but the house we were to live in was totally snowed in." They made many good friends and enjoyed a very active social life. Dora, who played the organ at church services, was even successful in organizing a choir, "complete with gowns and harmony." During the three years in Bonne Bay, Ted and Dora added two more daughters to their family: June ("born on the kitchen table with a very good midwife in attendance") and Margaret (Peggy), born in the hospital at Norris Point. (Another fourteen years would go by before the Russells would have a son.)

The three years they spent in Bonne Bay were very eventful for Newfoundland. The Second World War was brought very close to home with the loss of the *Caribou* in October 1941. Then in December 1942, news came about the Knights of Columbus fire in St. John's, about which Dora made the following entry in her diary (Wednesday, December 16, 1942): "A hundred people perished, many of whom were Canadian service men. A mass funeral was held yesterday afternoon… It was a pretty ghastly affair, from the stories we've heard of it." Dora kept in touch (by radio) with international as well as local news. Her diary is punctuated with brief allusions to events on the world stage: "Meeting announced last night at Casablanca - Roosevelt and Churchill" (January 7, 1943); "Germans are practically routed out of Stalingrad now" (February 7, 1943).

In July of 1943, Ted was offered the job of director of co-operatives with the Commission of Government. He accepted, and the family moved to St. John's, where both Ted and Dora would reside for the remainder of their lives. As soon as life returned to a semblance of normalcy, Dora began looking for a job. She records that in March 1944, she wrote a series of articles that she submitted to *The Daily News*. Response? "Too political for women's reading" and "Try something along the Dorothy Dix line." (Dorothy Dix was an American popular advice columnist and author of *How to Win and Hold a Husband.*) The precise subject matter of these articles is unknown, as none of them have surfaced.

A few months later she submitted a batch of articles (possibly the same ones) to *The Evening Telegram*. They were accepted. Dora took the next step, raising the question with the newspaper that "maybe they needed a woman's editor?" The newspaper's "A Page for Women" consisted of syndicated material on predictable subjects such as recipes, fashions and horoscopes. There was, however, no local news, and certainly no commentary. Dora's mission was successful. In spite of the fact that she had no formal training for such work, she was hired as *The Evening Telegram*'s first woman's editor.

For its time, this was indeed a significant achievement. Dora was looking for a job not out of economic necessity but for self-fulfillment and community contribution. For her, writing was in part an escape from the tedium of domestic duties, as well as years of living in restrictive environments. This job would be a gale of fresh air. Here she was - a married woman with four small children at home - actively pursuing a career. For the 1940s, this was heady stuff! Furthermore, the timing was perfect. The next three years would prove to be among the most tempestuous in Newfoundland's history. And Dora Russell would be in the thick of it.

St. John's in 1945 was a very different city from the one Dora had left ten years earlier. The war had brought prosperity, thanks in large part to the presence of both Canadian and American forces. The city's two major newspapers – *The Evening Telegram* and *The Daily News* – were thriving. Economic and social changes awakened intellectual activity, most notably in literature and the arts; a plethora of small periodicals and magazines gave new impetus to Newfoundland's creative spirit. A sense of pride began to re-emerge. Not surprisingly, this optimism extended to the political sphere, an optimism not seen nor felt since the loss of responsible government in 1934. The rhetoric that so characterized Newfoundland politics in days gone by began to resurface. Newfoundland was ready for a reassessment of its method of governance.

In December 1945, the British government announced the creation of a National Convention. The task of the convention was twofold: to consider and discuss the economic state of Newfoundland; and to make recommendations to the British government regarding possible future forms of government to be put to the people in a referendum. The election of forty-five delegates from thirty-eight districts took place in May of 1946. Of significance for the new woman's editor of *The Evening Telegram* was the fact that only two women offered themselves as candidates – without success. Deliberations began in September. Before long, the battle lines were drawn and the debates were bitter and divisive.

The convention recommended that two alternatives be put to the people: a return to responsible government, or the retention of the Commission. Delegate

Joseph R. Smallwood's motion that Confederation be included as a third option was defeated 29-16. But, following a massive campaign, the Confederates presented to Britain a petition with over 50,000 signatures. Consequently, Confederation with Canada was added to the ballot. The result of a referendum (June 3, 1948) was that restoration of responsible government received the most votes but fell short of the required majority. After weeks of acrimonious campaigning, a second referendum (July 22) resulted in a majority for Confederation with Canada. (Final count: Confederation - 78,323; responsible government - 71,334.)

Dora Russell covered the entire convention for *The Evening Telegram* in a column entitled "Proceedings of the National Convention." Those hours and days spent listening to the ongoing debates provided her with significant material for two columns for her Woman's Page: "The Woman's Angle" and "Spectatler." While her subject matter ranged across the social and economic spectrum, including topics such as playgrounds, roaming dogs, soap operas, slum housing and the cost of electricity, she was at her best in the columns that dealt with political issues. Her pro-Confederation bias did show through, even though *The Evening Telegram* itself was deliberately steering a neutral course (unlike *The Daily News* which was clearly pro-responsible government). Several readers engaged her in debate through the editorial page, including one of the leading proponents of responsible government - Albert B. Perlin, editor of *The Daily News* and author of the political column "In the News by the Wayfarer." Even the governor of Newfoundland, Sir Gordon Macdonald, read her material, quoting extensively from "Give us the Men" in his New Year's address on January 1, 1949.

Reading Dora's political columns, one gets a sense that she was in her glee, combining serious discussion with light satire and a cheeky charm. She consistently advocated for more women in the political arena, pointing out the unique qualities that females could bring to the table. In her "Spectatler" columns, she repeatedly returns to the fact that not one woman was elected as a delegate to the National Convention. She hoped, through her writing, that she could bolster enough self-confidence among women that they would be moved to participate in such events in the future.

Looking back through the lens of much intervening history, one could make the case that Dora Russell was a feminist. She was not one to attach labels to any one person or group. I have no doubt that she saw herself as an advocate for women; that she supported equality for women; that she wished to break down some of the stereotypes that existed in her time, especially about the working mother and the career woman; that she promoted and supported local women in all their endeavours, both domestic and public. She focused on serious issues from a woman's perspective and for the first time gave women a collective voice in the political process. She commented on the activities of women in the local community, valuing their work and their contributions. Finally, she cleared the way for other aspiring female journalists, including Grace Sparkes and Cassie Brown (*The Daily News*) and Sylvia Wigh (*The Evening Telegram*).

During 1948, Dora's participation in the political scene became more specific. She presented radio talks (on VOCM) in which she espoused the benefits of union with Canada. She contributed material to *The Confederate* (a propagandist tract). In fact, she became so closely involved with the Confederation campaign that any degree of objectivity was virtually impossible for her to retain. In the summer of 1948 she resigned her position at the newspaper and devoted her energies to the campaign. She did not, however, abandon her writing. She undertook four descriptive pieces about travel in Newfoundland for the *Atlantic Guardian*, beginning in September with "Around the Bay." Her commentary was accompanied by several photographs taken by Fred Ruggles.

In April 1949, Dora decided to act on her own political aspirations: she approached Smallwood about the possibility of being a candidate in the upcoming provincial election. She was interested in the district of Fogo (which included Change Islands). Smallwood flatly refused. "Joe decided that two in a family was too much," she wrote in her diary on April 28. (Her husband Ted had already been assigned Bonavista South). "I might not have got it anyway. Joe was afraid that women in politics was too revolutionary," mused Dora in her diary. Harold Horwood would later confirm that Smallwood had a "blind spot" when it came to women. Significantly, during his twenty-two years as premier, not one female candidate won a seat under the banner of his Liberal Party. One woman (Alma Badcock) ran for election in St. John's West (against John Crosbie) but was unsuccessful.

For Dora, perhaps Smallwood's rebuff was a good thing. She was a democratic socialist at heart and was attracted by the policies of the CCF.[1] She was one of the delegation that met M.J. Coldwell[2] at the airport when he came campaigning for the May 1949 federal election. A photograph of Dora meeting Coldwell appeared in *The Evening Telegram*. Her name was singled out as a potential candidate for the CCF in the federal election. "But there's just one thing against her," quoted a piece in the same newspaper. "Her husband is running as a Liberal candidate in the provincial election." So she lost out. She did, however, serve as a member of the Provincial Executive Council of the CCF until 1955.

Once Ted had been elected to the House of Assembly and then invited to join Smallwood's cabinet as minister of Natural Resources, Dora found herself in the social limelight. On the Government House invitation list for various state functions, she would attend a reception in honour of Princess Elizabeth and the Duke of Edinburgh. She loved the active social life. But in late March 1951, that all came crashing down, with Ted's resignation from cabinet and expulsion from the Liberal Party. She often spoke to me about those painful days, about former "friends" who no longer called or dropped by. Ted had difficulty finding gainful employment. Dora helped where she could: radio broadcasts, work with Dominion Statistics, etc. She always believed that deliberate attempts were made to shut potential employment doors in their faces. Nasty stuff about her

[1] The Co-operative Commonwealth Federation, Canada's first social democratic party, was formed in 1932. Its first leader was James Shaver Woodworth. The first CCF premier in Canada was Tommy Douglas. In 1961, the CCF was succeeded by the New Democratic Party with Douglas as its leader.

[2] Major James Coldwell (1888-1974) was the leader of the CCF from 1942 to 1960. "Major" was his first name, not a military title.

husband appeared in the local papers, especially *The Sunday Herald*. Even Dora's meeting with Coldwell was dredged up. Ted wrote in 1966: "Had I known what my resignation was to cost my family, I might conceivably have stayed on."

Dora had one more kick at the political cat in 1954. At the time she was giving regular reports on the proceedings of the House of Assembly on VOCM. Disturbed by the behaviour of Premier Smallwood, who made no attempt to hide his contempt for the press, she wrote a lengthy letter ("In Defense of Reporters") to the editor of *The Daily News*. She drew attention to the way Smallwood treated Harold Horwood, a former supporter-turned-critic, a victim of "an unwarranted blast of venomed spite," labelling him among other things "a loathsome literary rat."

In the meantime, Dora remained an active participant in the St. John's artistic community. A regular theatre-goer, she especially enjoyed the annual season of the London Theatre Company, founded in 1951 by Leslie Yeo and Hilary Vernon. A regular attendee at community concerts, she sang in the St. John's Glee Club as well as in St. Thomas's Church choir. She and Ted also had their fifth child, a son (Kelly), born in 1956.

With the exception of an occasional letter penned to an editor, Dora's writing after 1951 was non-political. She turned her attention to other genres, notably short stories, radio scripts and personal essays. Her first success was a short story, "The Whelping Ice." Her radio scripts, none of which have been published until now, include "Tidal Wave," "Story of a Street" and "The Bedlamer." She even tried her hand with a television script ("Second Mama"). She had better luck with her personal essays, two of which appeared in print: "Facts about our Superstitions" (*Here in Newfoundland*, May 1956) and "Labrador Wedding" (*Newfoundland Woman*, July 1964; August 1964).

During the late 1950s Dora revived her interest in astronomy, thanks in part to her daughter June, who, as a girl guide, suggested her mother as a person who could help her and other guides obtain their Astronomy badges. Motivated by this, Dora arranged with *The Evening Telegram* to write a series of columns entitled "All About Stars." She started them in 1959, continuing for close to ten years. She dug out all the old scrapbooks and notes, supplementing them with mountains of new material that had emerged in the interim. She even purchased a telescope. The columns were highly successful, in large part because she was able to make scientific material more accessible for the lay reader. And, with increasing interest world-wide in space during the decade leading up to the first moon landing, the material proved timely.

Dora was also a founding member of the St. John's Centre of the Royal Astronomical Society of Canada, serving as its president for four years. Her significant contribution was recognized in 1977 when she received two prestigious awards. One was the Queen's Medal, given on the occasion of the twenty-fifth anniversary of the accession to the throne of Queen Elizabeth II. The second was the RASC's Service Award, presented to her at the society's annual assembly in Toronto "In Recognition of Outstanding Service to the Society." Another ceremony was held locally at city hall, presided over by

St. John's Mayor Dorothy Wyatt and attended by several active members of the St. John's Centre of the RASC.

Dora's interest in astronomy continued until her death. Indeed, she was planning a book about the stars (entitled "The Fire-Folk"). Poor health plagued her, however, and the project made little headway. She died peacefully after a lengthy illness on February 9, 1986 at the age of seventy-three.

Dora Russell deserves to be rescued from obscurity. Determined to combine homemaking and child-rearing with a career in journalism, at the time not deemed appropriate, she proved very successful at both. An advocate for equal rights and opportunities for women, she challenged prevailing attitudes shaped by a patriarchal society, while at the same time respecting work done by women in more traditional fields of endeavour. A versatile writer, she drew on her many interests, guided always by a strong sense of social conscience, a devotion to family and the courage of her convictions.

Elizabeth Miller

PART I: THE "TELY" YEARS (1945-48)

Later in life, Dora Russell would comment that the years she spent at The Evening Telegram *were among her happiest. She was hired in 1945 as woman's editor, just a year after she and her husband Ted moved to St. John's from Woody Point, Bonne Bay. Dora would transform the newspaper's "A Page for Women" into a forum for discussion of a wide range of issues of interest to women (and, she hoped, men) from the traditional to the political – with a distinct preference for the latter. She accomplished this primarily through four regular columns: "The Woman's Angle," "Spectatler," "Woman of the Week" and "Day by Day."*

THE WOMAN'S ANGLE

"The Woman's Angle" was the anchor of The Evening Telegram*'s new look for its female readership. A daily editorial column, it gave Dora the opportunity to range over a wide variety of subject matter. She was, however, never far from political themes. As the decade moved along, Newfoundland found itself mired in political controversy: the National Convention; the struggle between supporters of responsible government and those of Confederation; the two referenda. This was grist for Dora's mill. Indeed, on more than one occasion she would find herself in the middle of the conflict.*

Not surprisingly, a recurring theme in these editorials was the absence of women in the political process. This was most apparent in the fact that of the forty-five representatives elected to the National Convention in 1946, not one of them was female.

GIVE US THE MEN

The progress of every community regardless of size depends on public spirited, unselfish leadership.

A country that cannot produce the men dare not face the responsibility of handling their own affairs. If a country cannot rise above its government, it would seem to be inviting disaster to put a body of men in power that we felt beforehand were not leaders in the best sense of the word.

However, it seems amazing that any Newfoundlander should insist that we have no capable men. We have plenty of men capable of taking over responsible government if given a fair chance in a self-supporting country or in a provincial government in event of Confederation. If we have not the men, we may as well "take a powder," for there will never be any future for this country under any form of government.

Were we not confident that we have men and women with the necessary zeal and honesty, we could not dare give further thought to the question of government other than to plead to England to do as she liked with us.

It is nothing less than insulting to a Newfoundlander to hear opinions expressed that "We have no men," especially to those among us who are capable and willing to assume the duties the country might require of them. If their efforts and intentions are so belittled, what chance have we of bringing our good men to the fore?

The need brings the man, and if to date men have been slow to come forward, it is because they prefer not to rush matters. It is because the hour has not yet come.

Consider for a moment the many men in this country who have for years given their time and energy to the public, the many men who have always been ready and willing to give contributions to worthy causes, the many who have attracted public recognition by their own efforts or have been leaders in their own particular groups. A man doesn't easily win the public's admiration, and when he does, there must be some sound reason for it.

No, we need not fear that we have no men. Rather need we fear that we have no other people capable of recognizing true worth, capable of discerning between a man zealous for his country's welfare and one who is out for his own gain. For if we had worthless men running the country in the past, the fault lies entirely with us for putting them there.

CITY MOTHERS A NECESSITY

Our City Fathers, no doubt, have the welfare of the city at heart, but that august body would benefit in no small measure from the addition to its ranks of City Mothers. The recent decision of the Municipal Council to use Bannerman Park for organized games provides an example of a measure that might not have been adopted had women been represented on the Council.

The north end of the park is to be used for organized games until such time as the Council can acquire a more appropriate site for the use of the youth of the city. It is true that the need of a playing field for organized games is acute, and that it is the duty of the Council to provide such facilities, but it is extremely regrettable that the smaller children should have to sacrifice any part of their park to the older children who wish to play softball and other games. Indeed, if organized games are to be played in the park at all, they should surely be of a nature to interest the smaller children.

Many mothers will regret this decision on the part of the Council, and it is likely that had there been feminine representatives on the Council, more support would have been given to Councillor Mews,[3] who was definitely opposed to the scheme proposed for Bannerman Park. The park has not only given great pleasure to under-privileged children who would otherwise be forced to play on the sidewalks and dusty streets of the city, but has proved a boon to thousands of mothers who like to take their babies and toddlers to the park for an afternoon's recreation.

The turning over of the north end of the park for organized games renders the surrounding area unsafe for mothers or children. Too much consideration has been given to the teenagers on this matter, and not enough to the small children and the mothers who have no suitable place to walk with their babies. The ruffled feelings of those mothers are by no means soothed by the promise of the Council to make this measure a temporary one, until such time as better facilities may be arranged.

Surely some such place can be found now as well as later? If not, the matter should lie until proper facilities can be found. Experience shows that these "temporary" measures have a distressing habit of remaining permanent.

Councillor Mews has the backing of many a mother when he says, "I do feel that a public park located in the

[3] Henry George Reginald Mews (1897-1982) served first as city councillor and later as mayor of St. John's (1949-65). He led the Progressive Conservative Party in the first provincial election (May 1949), losing to the Liberal Party under Joseph R. Smallwood.

city is not the place for organized games, unless it be for the kiddies." His objection to the playing of games in the park, he stated at last week's Council meeting, was actuated by the desire to ensure the safety of persons who have to frequent that section of the park. He thought that the present location of the softball diamond was detrimental to the safety of persons passing through the park, and in this matter his attitude was beyond criticism.

DEBATE A FIASCO

Women, let's not be discouraged. If we are dubious as to whether we could successfully run a debating society of our own, forget it! It would be impossible not to run a debate better than that which took place last Thursday at the MCLI.[4]

Two and a half hours were allotted in the discussion to the merits and demerits of representative and responsible government. Hundreds of citizens turned out under inclement walking conditions, spurred on by last week's animated debating, to hear, as they hoped, some new angle on a subject of vital interest to them.

Far from coming to any informal decision, however, we the public, "came in the self-same door through which we went."

One speaker spent most of his time explaining that he didn't really mean what he said the week before. Another venerable old gentleman spent at least a half hour on subjects other than those under discussion. Another speaker, however, although he said nothing very

[4] The Methodist College Literary Institute was a debating society in which many a Newfoundland politician honed his oratorical skills. Its presence ensured the survival of the tradition of public debate at a time when Newfoundland was without a legislative assembly.

eloquently, at least set the stage for further discussion by setting forth questions that, if taken up, would have livened up the debate. However, the mischief had already been done earlier in the evening, and this was already a lost cause.

Years ago, we remember setting out on one of the northern trails on dog-team.The team was pulling splendidly, and we were making great progress, until suddenly a little rabbit jumped in the path of the dogs, who forgot their objective completely and gave frenzied chase to the rabbit. At Thursday night's debate, the rabbit appeared when one speaker rose to denounce this country's manhood by insisting that we have no men capable of running the country. From then on, nine-tenths of the debate centered upon a discussion, not of representative and responsible government, but of the merits and demerits of the men we have now, the men who have gone before us, and the men who are coming after us.

Speaker after speaker rose to his feet to say very impressively something that had already been said, not once, but many times. A deluge of dates and historical events tumbled about our ears.

We were left with the opinion that, if our country has good men, they were not present at Thursday's orgy of heated contention. We are, furthermore, left with the opinion that if this debate is representative of our city's best thinkers, this country has a long hard road to travel and we tremble for its future.

LET ACTION SPEAK

We are readily touched by a pathetic story such as was recited at the last meeting of the City Council, drawing from Councillor Spratt[5] the observation that the tale would "touch a heart of stone."

A woman and her children had been thrown out of their house. For days the furniture lay on the sidewalk, covered with a piece of tarpaulin. The family had sought shelter in the police station, but on the advice of her clergyman, who thought such a life would have a detrimental effect upon the children, the mother succeeded in finding neighbours who were kind enough to take her children in. Neither the Government nor the GWVA,[6] when approached, could find accommodation for this family of a man who had been a victim of war. Their dismal plight remains unassisted.

Willing and able to pay rent, this woman was nevertheless forced to find shelter in the police station, and to eat meals in the park. What a blessing the recent fine weather must have been to her.

The futility of shaking our heads sympathetically over such a moving story should be apparent by this time. Let action speak louder than words. It has been said that the "war buildings" have proved unsuitable for use as homes for unfortunate people who lack accommodation, but surely such unsuitable buildings would prove a more desirable shelter than the police station and the park.

To say that accommodation cannot be found for this family is indeed to admit defeat. Accommodation must be found. In this respect, the Council no doubt finds

[5] James (Jimmy) Spratt served as a member of the St. John's City Council during the 1930s and 1940s. He had the dubious distinction of having a son (Herbert Spratt) convicted of murder and hanged in 1942. This was the last application of capital punishment in Newfoundland.
[6] The Great War Veterans Association.

difficulties in its path, but our councillors were chosen with the hope that difficulties would not daunt them. A way must be found to house not only this family whose story we have heard, but other families who find themselves in like predicament. This is probably not an isolated instance. There must be many such heartrending stories that have not been drawn to the attention of the public.

It would surely be preferable to live in a tent rather than expose young children to the humiliation of having to seek shelter in a police station and eat meals in a park. If all such unhappy people were to be drawn from the shocking conditions of over-crowdedness under which they live and given tents to live in, the sizable area those tents would cover would perhaps galvanize an over-pathetic citizenry into action. Those tents would stand, a shameful testimony to a generation that simply didn't bother to see that its brothers and sisters had a fair chance of becoming good and useful citizens.

MUSIC IN THE SCHOOLS

A teacher who evidenced considerable interest in music was curious to find out whether the average home in her community held any indication as to appreciation of music. Accordingly, she asked her pupils what instruments the family possessed. The results surprised her. Almost every home had one, two and sometimes three instruments, apart from the radio. There were accordions, organs, occasionally pianos, guitars, fiddles and banjos.

The people of this country have very little musical education, but a great love of music. Fishermen have gathered around on the wharves after a hard day's work, and have sung the fishing songs they love so well. The old-fashioned organ stands proudly in the most prominent corner of the parlour, stately even in disuse. An immense pride is taken in its possession, and great satisfaction is shown when understanding fingers drag out a melody from its ugly yellow cracked keys.

Newfoundlanders are music-hungry, and the fact that there is a reasonably wide distribution of musical instruments among families all over this country seems to indicate that here is a field of education almost untouched by the schools.

There is no subject that might be taught in the schools that would have so wide an influence and cultural value during hours of relaxation. Instruction in many of these instruments could be given by schools if they were equipped with teachers capable of giving such instruction. Unfortunately, Algebra and Latin seem to be given greater prominence in the school curriculum than the study of something that might make a worthwhile contribution to family life.

With so many instruments in the possession of the home the possibilities of a school orchestra become apparent. The initial expense in the form of instruments has already been met by the parent, and the remaining cost to the Department of Education would not be great. Teachers should be given an opportunity of learning as much of the rudiments of music as would enable them to stimulate interest in the communities.

Due to the necessity for individual attention, music to date has been confined only to those children living in the towns whose parents can afford to pay for tuition.

Time, however, may bring changes in respect of evolving a successful method of class teaching. In fact many communities in Canada provide classroom instruction with encouraging results, and for many years the musical educators of that country have urged the acceptance of the study of piano and other instruments in the schools.

NEW-FOUND-LAND

It is strange that after living in Newfoundland (off and on) for four and a half centuries, we, the people of Newfoundland, should disagree as to the pronunciation of our country's name. It is time for us to try to reach agreement on the subject.

The Americans, who accent the first syllable, and the British and Canadians, who accent the second, are obviously wrong. In any case we would like to know who are they that they should decide how or how not to pronounce our country's name. The pity of it is that even amongst ourselves, we differ. Why even the delegates to the National Convention pronounce Newfoundland in different ways, while foreigners, who are genuinely anxious to pronounce the word correctly, find it impossible to do so.

There are people who stoutly maintain that the name should be pronounced as three separate words - new, found, land - with equally strong accents on all three. The only thing wrong with this is that it simply can't be done. True, it is possible to do so while singing our National Ode, or in reciting a proclamation or intoning a prayer. Try it yourself, and see. Mr. Winston Churchill, who favours this pronunciation, can manage it when using the word in a public address, but to most of us in ordinary everyday language – it just can't be done. To pronounce the word with all syllables accented would mean taking time out whenever we reached the word in ordinary conversation, and going through a lingual gymnastic that would sound very unnatural.

Many think the correct pronunciation of "Newfoundland" is the pronunciation given by the common ordinary people in their common everyday task. A weak accent on the first syllable, no accent at all on the second, and a strong one on the third.

After all, who can better decide how to pronounce "Cholmondeley" than the people who live there? Why then, should we not agree to accept as correct the verdict of the vast majority of our people on the correct way of pronouncing the name of their country? Be assured that whatever pronunciation others may put on the word, to most people, it will always be "New-fn-land."

HERE ARE THE MEN – AND WOMEN

It is now apparent that all fears of apathy towards the National Convention, which might have resulted in inadequate and inferior representation, are groundless.

Nomination Day saw for the first time in fourteen years a faint tinge of the excitement that prevailed in the old days of competitive politics.

No less than 124 candidates have been nominated for the forty-two seats in the National Convention, with three districts yet to be heard from. Labrador, St. Barbe and White Bay districts are not yet in a position to nominate candidates, due to the delay in compiling the census in those districts.

The calibre of the citizens who have announced themselves is, in the main, a happy augury for the convention. In answer to the oft-put question – "Where are the men?" – here they are, 124 of them, drawn from all classes, creeds and ways of life, and possessed of a desire to do their level best for the good of the country. These men, if they have axes, can have little hope of grinding them at this convention.

The list of candidates is widely representative, embracing merchant, lawyer, housewife, labourer, teacher, salesman, clerk, former politician, writer, ex-serviceman, blacksmith, grocer, carpenter, doctor, trucker and accountant. Of particular interest to readers of this page is the fact that two women have come forward at this time. Mrs. Frances Holmes is contesting a seat in St. John's West, and Mrs. Martha Hann is standing for Humber district.[7]

With so many candidates eager to represent their country, the competition should be keen. There can be but little campaigning done, however, unless contestants wish to make a point of creating a platform for some particular form of government. This seems unlikely, as candidates undoubtedly realize that the peculiar requirements of the convention forestall any such method of campaigning.

It is difficult, therefore, to see how these candidates propose to "put themselves over" to the public, to whom many would-be representatives are mere names. The public must be in a position to form some sort of judgment as to the contestant's capabilities, so that some form of campaigning is surely necessary.

[7] Neither was successful in winning a seat.

We now have a little more than two weeks in which to decide which of the candidates we consider most worthy of assuming the responsibility the public wishes to give them by election to convention.

Interesting days lie ahead. Let us hope most sincerely that they will be used to the best advantage of this our country. Indeed, let us see to it, by electing the best representatives.

CONVENTION DRAWING NEAR

Next Wednesday will see the opening of the much talked of National Convention. The prime point of interest at the moment is the decision that body will come to regarding publicizing the meetings. Whatever the outcome, we must abide by it, since these are our delegates, elected by us because of the faith we have in their ability to do the best thing. No longer must we think of the convention in the cold terms of an organization. It is composed of living, breathing Newfoundlanders whose aim, we trust, is to give this country the best form of government.

Many have contended that the proceedings should be broadcast. It is difficult to see, however, how the convention can make this possible. Proceedings will be lengthy, and while at first, interest will be keen, the public would before long find itself content to listen to or read a simple resume of the day's work.

It has been rumoured that a certain member of the convention has already prepared a five-day speech. Men enjoy the importance that public speaking gives them, but for our part, we place more confidence in the man who sits quietly, assimilating the information and statistics placed before him, and occasionally finding his feet in order to make a short, pithy commentary. It should not take half an hour to state one simple fact or bring up one forceful argument.

The newspaper remains the most stable manner in which the convention may make its debates public. The public will not (or should not) be interested so much in the speeches as in the facts that are brought to light. These, every citizen should have a chance to hear, read and debate - on the streets, in the clubs and in the kitchens.

No doubt members of the public will be given the opportunity to attend sessions. Unfortunately only a small number will be able to be accommodated and many will likely be turned away. Many of us have never seen the inside of the Colonial Building nor the room in which the destiny of our country will be determined. An opportunity to do so would be a momentous one.

SEPTEMBER 11, 1946

A date to go down in Newfoundland history is today, which saw the opening of the National Convention.

Not until Friday, however, will the convention actually get down to business. This afternoon will be occupied with preliminaries after which the convention will adjourn until tomorrow afternoon when an address of loyalty to be presented to His Majesty the King will be moved and supported.

The nature of the convention is so unusual that its proceedings from that day on is still a matter of conjecture. No doubt its first duty will be to draw up a plan of procedure, a set of rules by which the meetings will conduct business.

The convention must come to a decision as to what steps will be taken to keep the public informed as to its debates and findings. It will want to know how far authority extends, and whether or not it is at liberty to summon any citizen or government head or expert on the country's affairs, for thorough questioning. These and many other details will have to be settled before the convention can get down to the work on hand, and proposals will have to be submitted regarding these considerations, to the meeting, which will undoubtedly debate the various points heartily before lending its approval.

To get a clear and concise picture of what is needed for this country, it will have to examine into the merits and demerits of our present system of government, of responsible and representative government, which forms we have had before. It will consider the feasibility of adopting a form of government as yet unfamiliar to Newfoundland. Besides these questions, it will examine minutely into the economic and financial position of the country, relating their findings to each system of government under consideration.

This done, a lengthy business, the convention will present its findings to the people of Newfoundland together with its advice as to the form of government the majority of members considers best for the country. Then will come the people's part, the vote.

Therefore, it is of interest to every citizen of this country, and to his children and children's children that he follow carefully the debates of convention, so that when the time comes for voting he will have clearer idea as to the issues involved and how they will affect him and his community. Such is the duty of the citizen.

As to the members of convention, the first elected body to sit in the House of Assembly since 1933, they are surely conscious of their great responsibility and of the honour the people have done in electing them to this most important work. It can never be too often stressed that these men hold the future of the island in their hands, and that the well-being of a quarter million people is depending on them.

OUR PLACE IS THERE

We do not wish to give the impression that proof is required of the fact that women's intelligence is as great as that of men. Facts speak for themselves, and many notable names might be quoted of women who have made a valuable contribution to the commercial, religious, economic, financial, professional, industrial and social life of their country.

Newfoundland women, however, have never taken the place they might in political life. The fear of inferiority hangs over them, resulting in an extreme reluctance to take any part in political discussions.

It is a regrettable fact that not one woman has taken a seat among the forty five members of the convention, to help in guiding the destinies of her country at such an important phase in its history, along the sanest and wisest path.

The fact that no woman sits on the convention, however, does not mean that the fair sex will fail to follow with considerable interest the course of the convention. Nor when the time comes for decision will a lack of knowledge of the salient facts prevent her from casting her vote wisely. As a matter of fact, women shine particularly well in this phase of thought, for they spent their lives comparing one thing with another, and adopting the course that seems wisest to them. There is no reason to fear that they will fail in their duty to their country.

Clare Boothe Luce, smart, well-groomed congresswoman of the United States, says in a recent issue of *Today's Woman* that she has never noted any difference between the qualities of the minds of her eight female colleagues in the House of Representatives, and those of their 400 male colleagues. She gives her reasons for this. First, these women enjoy absolute equality with men in their work. They get not only the same privileges, salaries and chances of advancement, but also meet with the same reception from the public.

Secondly, Luce offers the fact that these women have access at all times to the same sources for facts and information as the men do. "Whenever and wherever this condition of equality occurs," she says, "equality of pay, prestige and access to information, the brain power of the average man and the average woman is soon seen to be equal."

Perhaps the women of Newfoundland are not yet ready to assume political responsibility. Perhaps they are not even interested. Be that as it may, the absence of women on the National Convention is unfortunately conspicuous. More than that, the presence of a woman there was a duty. We have no one to represent our views or keep our interests in mind. The assembly is wholly masculine, a fact that reflects on our tardiness in coming forward to offer our services, and casts on us the slight of indifference.

FORGOTTEN LAND

There are many bays, points, capes and what-nots in Newfoundland, whose inhabitants have long since resigned themselves to being forgotten.Their extreme isolation renders it difficult to stretch out the helping hand, although the hand must not be withheld because of that.

Of all the instances of neglect that we might quote, none can with better reason be claimed to have been so completely forgotten as Labrador. In the eyes of most of us, Labrador is a wealthy land, and some day we hope to realize tremendous profits from its development. Seldom indeed, have we given a thought to the people of that area who are surely of greater importance than the land itself, valuable though it may be.

The Labradorians have put up with a great deal. Their distance from us, though not great in terms of miles, is great because of their isolation and the difficulties of communication for much of the year. Subsequently, if they grumble in their discontent, we hear little of it, and what we do hear we are prone to dismiss from our minds as of little account.

The feelings of Labradorians may well be imagined as they hear as they often do, the question discussed of the practicality or otherwise of selling them to another country, and of the gains we hope to make if we should keep Labrador in the hope of future development. Never a word about the people there, but always about the land and the richness.

As Mr. Keough[8] pointed out in his masterly address last week before the National Convention, we had never

[8] William Keough was a field worker with the Division of Co-operatives during the Commission of Government. An ardent Confederate and a persuasive speaker, he later served in the first provincial cabinet.

even thought of giving the vote to the Labradorians until the matter of elections for delegates to the convention came up. It remained for the Commission of Government to grant them that privilege, and one wonders, had we responsible government today, whether Labrador would yet have been suitably recognized.

So far we have shirked our responsibility to the people living there. No doubt they long to have their country opened up so that they might enjoy some of those benefits which other parts of Newfoundland have long enjoyed. But they must wonder who, in event of that development, would stand to gain, they or this island?

Their attitude as to future government may also be readily imagined. They have only to look across the border to where Canadian Labradorians are enjoying the comfort of warmer houses, cheaper and more nutritious food, and advantages of educational, health and public services. What they see there and what they observe about themselves and what they have to endure must make an odious comparison that can end only in their placing their weight in favour of Confederation.

SOAP OPERAS

Your mind isn't functioning if you agree with everything you read, even if we write it.

We don't expect our readers to agree with our criticism of soap operas, particularly as they seem to fill a popular need among women. Just why that is so, we never could understand, and our opinion is that women would enjoy a better type of radio if they were given it, contrary to a fact that we have often stressed, that the public always gets what it wants. However, perhaps in this instance, the public doesn't quite know what it wants, and takes what it is given with thankfulness that it can escape from the petty worries of everyday life by sympathizing with somebody else's petty worries instead.

For ourselves, however, we ought to want something better. There is nothing vicious about these soap operas. In that respect they are not to be compared with the comic sections read daily by our children, or the type of movie pictures they attend.

The soap opera is just plain silly, that's all, and we say that knowing we are probably stepping on the toes of a great many soap opera enthusiasts. A simple little incident is made to last over a broadcasting period of many hours. Action is completely dull, and the players' lines are dripping with a sickly, tiresome sentiment that makes one wonder what appeal the play can possibly make to a normal person.

There is no gainsaying the fact, however, that the appeal exists. The popularity of these stories speaks for itself. Thousands of Newfoundland housewives drop their dishwashing, or run in from hanging the clothes on the line, to find out how Jack made out after the removal of his appendix. Hundreds of domestics would leave their jobs flat if the mistress refused to allow them half an hour off every morning to follow the love adventures of Mary and her trials and tribulations.

Scores of housekeepers sit in the parlour at certain hours with their mixing bowl lying on their laps, intending not to waste a minute of the morning's work, but as the action wears on, the spoon lies neglected in the batter, and Madam Housekeeper permits a tear to steal from the corner of her eye. Poor Jean! She has so many troubles, and now on top of it all, her husband is leaving her. Such a little misunderstanding, too. If only Madam Housekeeper were on the spot, she would set things right so easily, because she would make it clear to James that sweet Jean had only his welfare and happiness in mind when she penned the fatal letter.

Women being the sentimentalists they are, it seems likely that the soap opera will always be with us. Fortunately, for us tougher members of the gentle sex, there are other programs, or there is the alternative of blessed quiet!

A CONVENTION OF WOMEN

From the very beginning, this column advocated strongly the election of women to the National Convention. Unfortunately, however, the voters didn't agree, and consequently we have a national assembly of men on the job.

We visited a public session a few days ago. We saw nothing, we heard nothing to change our belief that women should sit on the councils of the nation. In fact, we noted five good reasons why women are preferable to men, reasons that were formed through observation of the "doings" at the National Convention.

The first thing that impressed us was the steady procession of delegates from the Chamber to the anteroom, obviously for a quiet smoke. Women, in general, are non-smokers, and few of those who do smoke would find it impossible to wait until the sessions were over. Always providing that a rule were made forbidding the powdering of noses, this constant dribble of delegates to the anteroom would cease.

A point which struck us as pregnant with significance was the utter waste of man power as evidenced by the convention. If only men could knit! What a store of bootees, pullovers, cardigans, mitts and diamond-patterned socks would have been turned out since September 11th. These garments would not have been lost to the customers had an assembly of knitting women been at work, and we can guarantee that they would have missed no point in the proceedings, either, not even if they were doing a cable stitch. As it is, few find the delegates looking most pathetic in their idleness, glad of the invitation by some speaker to turn to paragraph seven, page three of the report.

Women have the reputation of being great talkers, but surely no woman can talk half as much or be so repetitive as so many of the men have demonstrated. They have the reputation of being too personal, but surely they couldn't be more personal than delegates who, not content with criticizing one another's arguments, have also begun to criticize the sound of one another's voices and the shape of one another's noses.

Well, that is a fray in which we could all join. We saw no less than three of the most atrocious ties you ever laid eyes on. Why didn't some delegate get up and put an end forever to this wearing of ties that upset one's artistic tastes?

Were women on that job, there would be far fewer delays than have been evident to date. They would be only too anxious to get home in order to put the beans in the oven, or drop in the fruit store to pick up some celery before going home. No, women do not enjoy the limelight. That, in point of fact, is why more women do not come forward in public life. They are content to hide their light under a bushel.

It might be argued that women have not the knowledge to enable them to play an intelligent part in the national deliberations.

But what knowledge? Our present delegates disagree on everything under the sun, including free trade versus protection, sending delegates away or not sending them, cross-country roads or local roads, etc, etc. Meanwhile, with all their debating, it is doubtful if any of them are convincing any of the others.

Maybe we will have learned a lesson from the convention by the time it has ended. Maybe future elections will find us more ready to support a woman candidate. At least we must agree that she could have done at least as good a job in this instance as the majority of the men.

TOURIST PROBLEM

Other countries are making extensive preparations for what is expected to be the biggest tourist year yet. What is being done to encourage travellers to wet their lines in Newfoundland rivers?

At this time of year, folks are culling through heaps of summer travel folders. Thousands of people who could not travel during the war are aching now for the tang of salt water. The United States travel agencies report that sailings are booked to Europe through July and that reservations are still piling up.

A summer tour of Europe is hardly the luxury today that it used to be. Hotel and transportation service is still disorganized and it will probably take five years before tourists receive first class catering.

Canada and the United States banking on this certainty are leaving no stones unturned to catch the tourist trade.They have lined up various domestic tours, ranging anywhere from a weekend outing to a month's vacation, and if you have the whole summer to spare, they are ready to take care of that for you, too. New resorts are being built to handle the expected flood of tourists.

We prate of the necessity of further production, yet we do nothing towards producing service for tourists. We talk of the need of new industries to help stabilize our shifting economy, yet we continue to neglect this possible source of revenues and employment.

The tourist trade cannot be expected to fall obligingly into our laps.We have to make efforts to attract the trade and we must have the planned means of holding it when we get it.

The resignation of the Tourist Board has thrown the onus of the tourist trade problem into the lap of the government. Surely a government which has successfully organized many of its schemes for the betterment of the country will not fail to measure up to the necessity of tackling the tourist problem in earnest.

WHAT SHALL WE DO WITH THE DRUNKEN DRIVER?

"Drunken drivers' parade" brings home to us the somewhat startling fact that we have in our midst many of these maniacs who, not content with risking their own lives, place the lives of those around them in jeopardy as well.

These are the "drunken drivers," an epithet that carries with it the length of scorn and disgust. If only the driver himself were running the risk, one might well shrug one's shoulders and marvel that anyone should choose this method of quitting the world prematurely. The drunken driver, however, becomes a heavy responsibility when his befuddled antics create a source of danger to innocent people.

There is a reason to regret the attitude of many drinkers, who claim boastfully that they can drive as well, even better, while drunk than when sober, that instinct serves at such a time in place of caution. A more absurd attitude is difficult to imagine. Instinct may tell the brain the right thing to do, but it cannot quicken the muscular action. It cannot guide hands and brain in the rapid action necessary to avoid disaster.

It should not be too difficult to keep the menace of drunken drivers off the roads. Grand Falls appears to be determined to do so, and we hear recently of fines being imposed by an indignant and responsible-minded magistrate to the tune of $150 plus loss of driver's license for six months for the first offence. The magistrate regretted that the law did not permit the imposition of a stiffer penalty.

If drivers cannot behave like rational human beings when at the wheel, they should not be permitted to drive at all. Stern action would soon bring them to their senses, and make the roads safe from their criminal disregard for public safety.

THE DOG HAS HAD HIS DAY

The dog problem which has occupied the mind of the City Fathers on so many occasions is once again to be solved.

No doubt the same energetic campaign against Fido will be undertaken, as has been evidenced in past efforts, and may be dropped just as energetically.

Long a top-ranking public nuisance, the dog has had too long a day. He has been monarch of every ashbin he has taken into his canine head to survey. Scarcely a lid that has not at some time or another been nosed from an ashcan. Not a street but that has at some point been strewn with the refuse from its houses.

But all that is to be changed. Now Fido will have his principal source of revenue cut off from him. The "three square meals a day" policy outlined by a delegate of the National Convention does not apply to Fido. He must seek what he may devour indoors.

The Dog Control Committee have laid their plans well, but this is a two-sided business. Without the co-operation of the dog owners the situation will not be relieved to any appreciable extent.

Dog owners hereby take notice that they must license their animals every year, and that they must not allow their dogs to roam about unchaperoned between the hours of 11 p.m. and 6 a.m. Any person who laughs off these regulations may not laugh off the fine - not exceeding five dollars - that will be imposed on the dog owner who breaks them.

Any domestic animal, in fact, found roaming the streets at large may easily find itself picked up by an impounder and kept under strict surveillance. He may be kept in the pound (the dog, that is). If not claimed, he will be offered for sale, or destroyed. If claimed, the owner must pay the impounding fees and any other expenses.

From all this, it would seem that the dog indeed has had his day. Lovers of animals will, if they continue to value Fido's companionship, pay strict attention to his comings and goings - or else.

It is indeed time that a vigorous policy be pursued with regard to the dog nuisance, which amounts in this country almost to a plague. St. John's is not alone in wishing its canine population under control. There are probably more dogs in Newfoundland than in any other country of its size. Outports are swarming with them, for here, the dog is necessary for hauling wood and providing a means of transportation. However, there is not as much trouble with dog control as there is in the city, because the owners are more conscious of their responsibility should their dogs break loose and kill hens and sheep. While there are many places where dogs are permitted to roam at large both day and night, the majority of settlements are trying to resolve the problem.

NEWFOUNDLAND UNIVERSITY

It seems impossible to conceive of any reason why we should not have a national university. Memorial College is at present equipped to give three years of university equivalent to those of any other university, and an additional year would permit students to receive their degrees here instead of taking themselves and their money out of the country. We confess to some bewilderment over the delay in raising Memorial University College to a degree-granting status.

The nature of the degrees the university would give at first would be limited, but would increase in time.

Degrees in Arts and Science and Law could be given, and later, Medicine, Biology and so on.

The comparatively small province of Nova Scotia has several universities, some of which have absorbed students from Newfoundland who have been unable to complete their studies in their native land. It has been very evident of late that Canadian universities have been pathetically eager to get our students. Why? Is it because our students are smarter or Memorial University College training is better? Or both?

If Memorial College were to be raised to the status of a full-fledged university, it is certain that it would become a focal point for the generosity of our wealthier citizens, who have always shown themselves to be alive in their responsibilities in this regard. Proof of this may be seen in the press today, as witness the advertisements for the Kellogg and Doyle scholarships. There is also the Pratt scholarship and others. Nor does the generosity of these citizens run entirely to scholarships. In every educational need, they are right to the fore, and have made possible a fuller education for our youth. There would be no lack of men to endow a chair, donate equipment, or lend financial assistance in other ways. There would be other scholarships offered for the whole courses, instead of for two years. Of that we have no good reason to doubt.

What better time to set the machinery going than in this year of national significance, when we are making a special effort to mark the 450th year of our national life? Why wait longer for the university that would fill the needs of our students, and keep Newfoundland money circulating in Newfoundland?

A DREAM OF FAIR WOMEN

Sitting through Monday's lengthy sessions of the National Convention, your columnist had a dream, a very pleasant dream.

It was a dream of fair women.

The countenances of forty-five very perplexed masculine faces faded away to a picture of forty-five women guiding the destinies of their country in the same impartial and earnest spirit with which they guide the destinies of their young.

When men bicker, they take great care to do it in such a gentlemanly way that it is not easy to pin the blame on them.They come back with reasons, carefully thought out reasons that have but one object, to get themselves out of the mess they have created, without any blame being attached to them.

Would an assembly of forty-five women sitting in the convention chamber have taken all of a week to make up their minds whether they wanted a delegation to proceed to Ottawa to seek terms *now* or *later*? The whole of the debate boiled down to nothing more than this simple fact, and forty-five men took a week to make up their minds.

Furthermore, when they had made up their minds, they could not put their wishes into effect, because first, every man had to have his say. It did not matter a row of beans that thirty other men had said exactly the same thing. Every voice had to be raised, not once but in many cases twice or thrice. It was this factor that placed the debate on the low level to which it sank.

Ladies, take heart! Shed your inferiority complexes, and know as of now, that any forty-five women in this country would not, could not, make such a fiasco of a debate as has been made of the Confederation delegation issue.

AH – MEN

A year or so ago we first stated that the convention would have been better off if a few women delegates had been elected to it. Today we have changed our mind. As we watched the close of the debate on the Smallwood motion, we felt that the convention would have been better if there had been *all* women delegates on it.

Women are popularly supposed to be illogical. But where in the world would you find any women so illogical as the delegates showed themselves to be? Orator after orator pleaded for the return to Newfoundland of their God-given right to decide their own destinies. Those same orators pleaded against and voted against the right of these same Newfoundlanders to decide whether they wanted Confederation or not.

Women are supposed to be stubborn. It is said (by men) that women stick to their opinions in spite of all arguments. But where in the world could you find women as stubborn as those men proved themselves to be? Two months ago, over a Bradley[9] motion, they lined up 29 against 16. The debate on the final Smallwood motion was a good one. It was lively, eloquent and thorough. But did a single one of those men change his opinion? Not at all. There they are, at the end, each man stubbornly hanging to opinions that had been ripped to

[9] F. Gordon Bradley (1886-1966) was elected to the National Convention in 1946 and served for a time as its chairman. He helped negotiate the terms of union with Canada. After Confederation, he served first in the House of Commons (as member for Bonavista-Twillingate) and later in the Senate.

shreds by his opponents time and time again. They ended 29 to 16. What a record for any convention of stubborn women to aim at!

Women are supposed to lack respect for facts and figures (statistical ones, we mean). But those men disagreed more widely than women could ever do. One moment a figure was 20 million, the next it was 70 or 80 million. One day, we would have divorce and state schools, the next we would have none of these things. And so it went.

Some suggest that women are inferior to men in their sense of fair play. But, be it noted that every advocate of responsible government voted not only against Confederation, but also against giving Confederates the right to vote for their preferred form of government. Women couldn't possibly be as unfair as that.

Nor could they be so illogical, or so stubborn, or show such utter disregard for facts.

FICTIONAL CHARACTERS

We were amazed on picking up yesterday's *Daily News*, to find that we were given a pat on the back by Wayfarer[10] for agreeing with his argument that Confederation should not go on the ballot paper.

When, we puzzled, did we argue that? Then, a light dawned with the realization that the widely-read columnist was confusing our opinion with that expressed by Mr. Bloggs, a character in Saturday's "Spectatler" who sometimes very timidly advances an opinion.

[10] Albert B. Perlin (1901-1978), columnist and editorial writer for *The Daily News*, used "The Wayfarer" as the byline for his regular feature, "In the News." His columns from 1946-49 offered readers an analytical response to the Confederation debate. He was a staunch supporter of a return to responsible government.

It is rather surprising that a seasoned newspaperman like Wayfarer should seize upon an opinion expressed by a fictional character, and attribute that opinion to the writer. Obviously it would be absurd to argue that the opinions expressed by other fictional characters in this weekly column are necessarily the opinion of the writer, who appears to be making an honest effort to present all sides. Mrs. Bloggs, Mr. Bloggs and Mr. Average Citizen seldom agree on anything. Even that embodiment of a good listener, Portia, sometimes throws in an argument when she isn't busy agreeing with the variety of opinions flung in her direction.

Any page is apt to become dull if the columnist and the editor insist on playing a little game of "Me Too." It can hardly be said that the Woman's Page of *The Evening Telegram* falls into that error. Indeed, we venture to say that in no newspaper in the country is such freedom of thought and difference of opinion so liberally permitted expression as may be found on this page. This is, of course, consistent with the unbiased attitude of this paper, whose desire it is to assist the people in a better understanding of *all* aspects of the problems confronting us, rather than favour one form of government to the exclusion of all others.

SPECTATLER

Concurrent with "The Woman's Angle" Dora wrote a second column (twice a week) dealing with similar subject matter. Its name is derived from The Spectator *(Joseph Addison) and* Tatler *(Richard Steele), two early 18th century British publications. Like her predecessors, she adopted a fictitious narrator (Portia) and created a cast of characters who inhabited her world, including Mrs. Haughty, Mr. Average Citizen and Mr. Livyer. This allowed her to add dialogue and debate, satire and wit, injecting new energy into the political material. Her main character was Mrs. Bloggs, a political enthusiast who ran for (and won) a seat at the National Convention. Of course, this was pure fancy, as no woman had been elected.*

ENCOUNTER ON THE STREETCAR

It was pretty stormy the afternoon I met Mr. Average Citizen and the streetcar[11] was crowded. We were both standing and hanging on as best we could.

"Hi, Portia," he said, gasping out the last word as a lady jabbed her pocketbook into his ribs.

"Hello, Average. You've heard the news, of course. What do you think of it?"

"No, what news? I didn't hear any news."

"You know you did," I accused. "The papers are full of it. I mean the news about our political future."

"No, can't say that I did. Must have missed it. What is it?"

[11] The St. John's streetcar system operated from 1900 until 1948.

I couldn't help wondering whether Average was being purposefully stupid or whether he was just plain cranky. It was a day to make anyone cranky, with all the wind and snow and the slowness of the traffic. However, I thought I'd overlook it.

"I mean about the convention next spring and our choice of government," I ventured.

"Shucks, Portia, that's not news. Britain promised us that several years ago. It's not news when Britain keeps her promises. She always keeps them. Some people think sometimes that she won't."

"Well anyway, Average, it looks like we're going to be rid of them, at long last."

"Who's going to be rid of which?"

I began to feel irritated. It always annoys me when men ask silly questions. "We're going to be rid of Commission Government, of course."

In my annoyance I had spoken rather loudly and heads began to turn my way.

"Are we?" he said. "I didn't know. Who says we are?"

"Well, it says in some of the papers that we are."

"Trouble with some of the papers, Portia, is that too often they say what they think themselves instead of trying to find out what the people think. Britain promised to give back self-government when we were self-supporting and when we asked for it. The convention is going to give us a chance to ask for it."

"And perhaps we won't ask for it," remarked a man standing next to him.

"But at least," put in another, "you'll admit we're self-supporting."

"Are we?" said Average. "I didn't know. Oh by the way,

Portia, my little fellow Jimmy – he's just five years old – picked up a ten dollar bill yesterday. I let him keep it."

"Sensible," I said. "But you're changing the subject."

"No, I'm not. Know what Jimmy said at dinner today? Said he was now self-supporting, earning more money than Pop. Thinking about going to Florida."

"The silly child. But he's just a child. He's bright enough, though, and I suppose in a few years from now he will be supporting himself. But of course it was just pure luck that he picked up a ten dollar bill. He can't expect to do that every day, can he?"

"Exactly," said Average, as he pressed the button, touched his hat, and pushed his way out.

WHAT MRS. BLOGGS KNOWS

We sat before the comfortable fire in Mrs. Bloggs' living room, cracking nuts and sipping her damson wine which she puts up herself every fall. Outside, a high wind romped endlessly with the listless snowflakes but inside it was cosy and Christmassy with the firelight on the trees and the feeling of peace and serenity that I always found in her home.

We sat munching, saying nothing. Mrs. Bloggs picked up the mitts she was knitting.

"Ah me!" she sighed, "I'd like to be on that convention in the spring."

"You would?" I asked, surprised. "Why? What would you know about such things?"

"Nothing," she answered, knitting away.

There were lots of answers I could have made to that, but I didn't wish to be impolite. She looked at me, and I knew she read what was on my mind.

"The fact that I'd know nothing about it," she said, wagging a knitting needle in my face, "makes me a perfect choice."

I took a piece of Christmas cake and munched it slowly. It tasted delicious, even without frosting. I was prepared to battle the point.

"What do you think about Newfoundland establishing its own currency?" I asked.

"I don't know," she answered.

"Nor I," I continued, determined that she should see her unsuitability for debating at the convention. "Give up our present system of taxation and derive our revenue from income taxes instead?"

"I don't know."

"Nor I. Do you think we should spend our nice fat surplus of 20 million dollars on highroads so that our country would be opened to the tourist trade?"

"I don't know."

"Nor I."

"And that guy Taplow doesn't know either," she said, "because he takes too many whiskies, and sits there all the time with his pipe and his newspaper and his whisky-and-soda."

Perhaps it was the reference to the glass that did it. I found myself reaching over to fill mine again with the delicious damson wine.

I settled back, feeling that I had shown Mrs. Bloggs quite clearly that no person knowing as little could possibly sit on the convention and do a good job.

"But," she said, "if I were in on that conference I would know, because I'd just sit there and wait until someone explained it to me. I'd stay there a year if I had to, but I'd find the right answers.

"That's why I say," she continued, "that the people who know the least are the best ones to have at that convention. People who already know the answers are no good to us. They haven't got open minds. They're so sure they know the right thing to do that they won't even stop to think that there might be a better way.

"And that's why I'd be a useful person to be there, because I don't know, and I know that I don't know. But I'd find out."

MEET MR. LIVYER

A day like Victory Day is one of those times when one meets people one hasn't seen in years.

I was admiring the way our Service girls were smartly singing along in the Big Parade, when I felt a jolt at my elbow.

"Why, Mr. Livyer," I gasped. "You here! Right from the Labrador! How are you?"

I was so glad to see him and had so many questions to ask him that I let a float pass by without so much as a glance.

Naturally, I was very curious about his part of the world. Labrador always seems so remote, so different from Newfoundland.

"Do you really live down there all the year through?" I wanted to know.

"That's why they call us 'livyers,'" he explained, as if there were some disgrace attached to it.

"I knew people fished there in season," I admitted, "but I haven't given much thought to the people who actually live there. What's it like? Are the people all of British descent?"

Mr. Livyer looked at me almost distastefully.

"Same race, same blood. And life is much the same there as in any other Newfoundland outport. People fish, tend their gardens, raise their livestock, same as anywhere else."

"And how about the convention?" I wanted to know. "I suppose there's not much interest in it?"

"Well," he replied with a smile, "we have four nominees, you know."

"Oh then there definitely is some interest."

"Of course. Remember, it's the first time in history that the people of Labrador have been invited to have any say at all in their own affairs," he said.

"They must consider it a great privilege?"

"It could be - if..."

"If what?" I asked.

"If the convention holds off long enough to include us. We're afraid we are going to get left out of it. Judging from what I heard on the radio and read in the newspapers, as soon as Election Day is over, there's going to be a demand that the convention start its meetings as quickly as possible.

"We don't know when our Election Day will take place but it will certainly take all summer to cover our vast coastline. And there's going to be some impatience, especially among the leaders who favour responsible government, to hold the convention right away."

"Oh, but they mustn't do that," I protested. "That certainly would not be fair. The convention cannot possibly go on until Labrador is ready too. But what did you mean that those wanting responsible government are likely to agitate for an early start?"

"Because," he responded, "it might not be to their advantage to have Labrador represented. You see, there's a Confederation element in Labrador as elsewhere.

"We had no say when there was responsible government. We've heard our future discussed by people who know nothing of our land, and we had no say. This time we do want a say."

I asked, "Do the people of Labrador favour any particular form of government?"

"Whoever is elected will represent the views of the people of Labrador," was his non-committal answer.

"There are some who think that people who live in isolated areas must pay the price of their isolation."

"We do that, sister," he returned grimly. "But since when has living in isolated areas meant that these people must be deprived of their rights?"

AVERAGE WANTS A HOUSE

"Good gracious!" I exclaimed, as I caught sight of Average's gloomy face. "Whatever's wrong? Is Mrs. Average sick?"

"No, she's not sick. But she will be when I tell her the news."

"Oh, have you had bad news? I'm so sorry. If there's anything I can do –"

"No, there's nothing you can do unless you are pal enough to die and leave me some money."

"Money!" I laughed, relieved. "Is that all? Why for a moment I thought – "

"Money, is that all?" mimicked Average. "Well, if you can't put me in the way of a few thousand dollars, perhaps you can put me in the way of a house - one that I can afford to buy, I mean."

"Oh," I said. "You've been looking into the houses the Housing Corporation is offering for sale. Is that it?"

Average nodded.

"And you're disappointed?"

Average didn't even bother to nod. "Oh I know," he admitted, "the houses are wonderfully compact, modern and well built. I know they'll cost very little to maintain and that the cost of heating will not be great. The foundations are so solid and the houses so well built that they'll last for generations."

"You're interested in buying, then?" I queried.

"Sure, I'm interested in buying. Look at the high rent we are now paying. Besides, we have to get out pretty soon and I don't see where we are to go. I counted on one of those houses."

"But surely," I protested. "If it's the money you're thinking of, you might be able to reach on one of them. After all, the terms are lenient. Your application will be considered on its merits, and when your situation is learned, you may get preference over other people who may be able to pay down twice as much and are not so badly in need."

Average gave me a sarcastic look. "You know the size of my family," he said. "I'd have to take the biggest house they have to offer."

"Yes?"

"And that will cost me $11,500. That's a steep figure for a man of average means."

"Yes, but you'll be paying it off in monthly installments. It'll be like paying rent to yourself. And there are other considerations. You'll have a house equipped with an oil furnace."

"And a fully equipped bathroom," added Average.

"And grand sinks, one deep for washing."

"And built-in kitchen cabinets."

"And double sashes and storm windows."

"And even fly screens."

"You have to take all of these into account when considering the cost of the house," I reminded him.

"Yes, but you also have to take the money into account. Might seem strange to you, but being a woman you probably don't consider those minor details."

I could cheerfully have kicked him. But he was so utterly downcast that I didn't have the heart. Besides, I was wearing my new brown and white loafers.

"$11,500 is bad enough," Average continued. "But that's not all."

"What do you mean, not all?"

"The land is extra. I'll have to pay $950 for the land and the cost of utilities."

"Why, that's a total of $12,450," I exclaimed.

Average looked at me mournfully.

"Why, you poor thing," I replied with compassion. "You are in a jam."

WE BOOST OUR SEX

It was late as Mrs. Bloggs and I were heading home after the second show. We had just seen *The Bells of St. Mary's*.[12]

[12] Released in 1945, this film starred Bing Crosby and Ingrid Bergman.

"You know," I said, hunching my shoulders against the chill of the early morning, "women are much better actresses than men."

"Naturally," returned Mrs. Bloggs dryly.

"Oh, you know what I mean," I laughed. "Women are better actresses than men are actors, if you insist on precision."

"I believe they are," she agreed. "When you consider Greer Garson's performance in *Random Harvest*, and then Bergman is always worth seeing. I doubt if there is a male actor who can equal the performance these women give."

"Nice to have you agree with me on something," I said. "But why do you suppose women can act better than men? The top writers are men, the best painters and designers are men. Why, men are even better cooks than women, since the world's finest chefs are male."

"Give us time," Mrs. Bloggs interrupted. "After all, experience does count for something, you know, and men have had countless generations of it behind them. We have hardly made a start yet. Give us time. Then consider that most women prefer doing a good job in their homes to making a career for themselves."

"You haven't answered my question, Mrs. Bloggs. Why do women act better than men?"

"That's easy," she said with a note of contempt. "I should think, Portia, you'd see that one for yourself. Women have a finer perception of things than men. They don't just play a part. They know what it's all about. They use their hearts as well as their heads."

We walked along in silence for a while. Then, "You know," said Mrs. Bloggs, "the way I see it, it's a great pity that women are not figuring more in the peace conferences. Men are not fighting for world peace at these conferences. They are fighting for political power. But if women's voices were raised and their opinions were listened to with respect, there'd be a real fight for peace. I'm telling you, men are too – "

"I think the word you want is 'nationalistic,'" I chimed in.

"Too nationalistic. That's it. They think in terms of their own country when they should be thinking of what's best for the whole world. They just dote on being looked up to as men fighting for their country's rights."

"Wouldn't women take a similar stand?" I asked.

"Not on your life," she emphasized. "Women have greater perception than men, like I said when we were talking about acting. They're all mothers at heart and they want what's best for their children and their neighbours' children. They think in broader terms than nationalism.

"Property! Boundary rights!" she went on, working herself up as she talked. "Tommyrot! A ghastly waste of time! Surely to goodness, human interests should come before political ones. That, my dear, is where our pompous, speech-making 'better halves' let us down. What we need is the personal view that women can bring. Heads are not enough. We need hearts as well."

"I have no doubt that you're right," I replied. "But if what you say is true, then it's not only the men who are letting us down. We are letting the world down ourselves. If we can make a worthwhile contribution, why aren't we pitching in?"

"I've no argument with that," returned Mrs. Bloggs. "You'll see Newfoundland come out of the fog when she has more women involved in politics. A woman at the convention would be a small step, but it's one that has to be taken. I'm all for any woman who has the nerve to take it on."

Trust Mrs. Bloggs to twist a subject around to the convention.

MRS. BLOGGS MAKES READY

I was sitting under the dryer when Mrs. Bloggs came into the beauty parlour. I overheard her making an appointment for Tuesday afternoon.

"Oh," I laughed, "so you're getting all dolled up for the opening of the National Convention. You're determined to look pretty, aren't you? Well, being the only woman delegate, maybe you will look pretty!"

She laughed good-naturedly. "A woman feels better and works better when she's looking her best," was her comment.

"Tell me," I said. "Don't you feel sort of excited, being so important a person as to sit on the National Convention?"

"No," she answered, seriously. "The delegate who sits on the convention is not the important person. It's the people for whom he or she is working. I look upon myself as nothing more than a channel through which information will travel. I shall assimilate as much of it as I can. I shall cast my vote as wisely as I can. I am promoting the welfare of the people who had enough confidence in me to give me their votes. Mind you, I may let them down, but it won't be because I am thinking of myself. It will be because I may perhaps arrive at the wrong decision."

"If you do," I interjected, "it won't be your fault."

"You know," she said, "it's been on my mind all summer. I'm too much on the shy side when it comes to giving an opinion in the presence of so many male delegates."

"For goodness sake, don't let that get to you. You don't know men. I mean it. Men are more broadminded than you think when it comes to women in government. You can't blame them for thinking that women are not very capable in matters political. We have yet to prove ourselves. Mrs. Bloggs, you just keep that in mind whenever you feel your arguments may be brushed aside just because you are a woman.

"Men," I continued, warming up to my subject, "respect other people's opinions. You'll find that you will be listened to, even if your opinions have no value. After all, consider the silly arguments you often hear men put forth. In fact, most of the hot debates we've heard ever since the convention was first talked of were put up by men - and I'm sure you can see plenty of discrepancies in them."

"Well," sighed Mrs. Bloggs, "I think you are talking plain common sense, but it just doesn't help. Tom gives me pep talks regularly but it's no good. Guess it's just a case of plain stage-fright."

"Nonsense," I scoffed. "Why, you know Percy Pulverize. You know the sort of arguments he puts up, and I've heard you tear them all to shreds."

"But I don't want it that way," she protested. "I hate to think of the convention deteriorating into a series of hot arguments. Percy will waste more time than enough without me jumping into the fray. No, that's not my idea of it at all."

"What is your idea of it, then?" I inquired.

"I hardly know myself," Mrs. Bloggs confessed. "I have a vague idea that we delegates should work together instead of preparing argumentative speeches. I think no one should have a word to say unless beforehand he examines the facts and ensures that he does not argue in favour of something that cannot work. We cannot afford wishful thinking. Our cards must be there on the table, for all to read."

MRS. BLOGGS AT THE CONVENTION

I couldn't resist running over to see Mrs. Bloggs after Thursday's session of the convention. I had attended the opening on the day before. In fact, our Culture Club went en masse. Mrs. Haughty, Mrs. Average Citizen, Miss Glamourpuss, all of us were there to see the doings and to give Mrs. Bloggs the benefit of our loyal backing. She nodded to us as she sat behind her smooth-looking desk, and immediately the placard on its surface hid her short frame from view.

She was looking tired when I went in to have a chat with her. "Can't sleep anymore," she said. "Nobody'll ever know what I am giving to my country!"

I laughed with her. "It'll be different when you get used to it," I comforted her. "Besides, you look so cute among all these men." She glared at me with good humour.

"I see Mr. Smallwood has started the ball rolling with his questions on the airport," I remarked.

"And very important questions they are too," she nodded. "If we are to examine our financial position, bearing in mind the extent to which the wartime boom has affected us, these questions on Gander will need to be taken very seriously."

"And then, Mr. Cashin[13] seems to be interested in the financial aspect of things."

"He always has been," returned Mrs. Bloggs.

"Were you very much surprised to find that the convention had no power to summon witnesses before it?"

"Well, no," she answered. "It has always been questionable whether that would be permitted or not. We still don't know and it may take quite a while to settle the question satisfactorily. Naturally we feel that we should have that right. But in any case, it is difficult to imagine any Newfoundlander refusing to bow to a request from the convention to appear before it and give any necessary information. If we can't do that, we can't do much. How can we determine whether the country can be self-supporting if we can't get the facts and figures?"

"You can't do it," I agreed. "But if you have no legal right to summon, there may be snags. For instance, a government employee may want to help the convention by appearing, but just suppose his department head refuses to allow him to appear. What then?"

"If he's a real Newfoundlander he will come anyway," Mrs. Bloggs replied firmly. "Now Portia, an old friend like you won't mind if I say I'm tired. I wish you would go home."

[13] Major Peter Cashin was a harsh critic of the Commission of Government and a fiery orator. Elected to the National Convention, he proved to be the most vocal of the advocates of responsible government.

I went home.

N.B. We wish to have it clearly understood that Mrs. Bloggs is a purely fictional character, and does not actually sit on the National Convention. She is rather a symbol of the representation of women that we would like to have seen on the convention.

CONFEDERATION AND MOSQUITOES

Mr. and Mrs. Bloggs and yours truly were finishing our lunch by the side of the road. Our pails were full of blueberries and Mr. Bloggs' 1925 Model T was waiting patiently to take us back to town.

"There's that mosquito again, Bloggs," exclaimed Mrs. Bloggs. "There, look, behind your left ear."

Mr. Bloggs dutifully slapped - and missed. "Drat the thing," said he. "That's the same mosquito that's been bothering me the last half hour. I'm going to give him a name - *The Confederation issue*."

"For goodness sake, Bloggs," reprimanded his wife. "Are you crazy?"

"Oh Mr. Bloggs," I interrupted. "Do tell me why."

Mr. Bloggs scratched the spot behind his ear.

"It's like this," he said slowly. "You take this Confederation business. It's like that mosquito in many ways. You can drive it away as often as you like, but it comes buzzing back. We've driven it away twice and here it is, as pesky as ever. Even this referendum that you women are talking about won't settle it."

I saw Mrs. Bloggs' mouth opening and hastened to beat her to it. "Don't interrupt, Mrs. Bloggs," I pleaded. "Go on, Mr. Bloggs. What were you going to say about the referendum?"

"The referendum," explained Mr. Bloggs, "favours Confederation at the expense of the other two. If commission is defeated, it is finished once and for all. If responsible government is defeated, it's finished too. That is, unless the commission wins. That would give everyone another chance in about ten years' time."

"But if Confederation is defeated," I prompted, "won't it be finished too?"

"Not on our life," retorted Mr. Bloggs. "It's like playing a game of 'heads I win, tails let's toss again.' It's like playing a game of baseball where the players on one side take one strike while the others take three. It's like this dratted mosquito," he continued as he made another energetic but futile slap. "It will be back again a few months later, even if it is defeated, and buzzing as loudly as ever."

"But what can be done about it?" I asked as we started towards the car.

Mr. Bloggs rubbed his mosquito bite thoughtfully. "For my part," he answered, "I'm not sure it should be allowed on the ballot paper at all. If it goes there, it should certainly not be declared the winner unless a clear majority of electors vote for it. If it is defeated, the issue should be buried for at least twenty years. Drat! There's that mosquito at me again," he grunted as he gave another slap. "Should have brought my fly oil. I've got my own special mixture, guaranteed to keep all mosquitoes away."

"I suppose you've even got a name for your fly oil?" I kidded him.

He nodded, and favoured me with a wink. "I think I'll call it *patriotism*," he said.

Mrs. Bloggs had been glaring ominously at her usually meek husband. "Bloggs!" she burst out with the fine oratory that won her applause in the convention chamber. "How dare you compare a great political issue with the tossing of a coin or the swinging of a baseball bat? How dare you speak of a national referendum as being unfair? How can you belittle the free expression – "

By this time Mr. Bloggs had pressed the starter, and the infernal din of his ancient motor drowned out all possibilities for further conversation.

"Wait until I get home!" shouted Mrs. Bloggs in my ear. But if he heard at all, Mr. Bloggs smiled placidly. Aided and abetted by his motor, for once he was having the last word.

MRS. BLOGGS AND THE PETITION

The doorbell rang. And, as I opened it, a chill icy blast blew in – and with it, Mrs. Bloggs.

"Dear me," she exclaimed. "It's really cold tonight, isn't it?"

"It sure is," I agreed. "I'm surprised to see you out on a night like this. I should have thought you'd be happier in your cosy living room at home."

"Not," Mrs. Bloggs firmly, "when there's work to be done."

"Why, Mrs. Bloggs, what work can you possibly have that takes you out on a night like this?"

"This, my dear," she said, flourishing a piece of paper under my eyes.

"What is it?" I asked.

"It's a petition," she answered. "You know, the petition to include Confederation on the ballot paper. And Portia, you must sign your name to it."

"Oh I must, must I?" I replied in amusement. "Well, what if I refuse?"

"You can't refuse."

"But surely you don't expect me to sign just because you're a friend of mine?"

"Of course not," came her retort. "I expect you to sign because it's the only sensible thing you can do."

"How are you getting on with it?" I asked, changing the subject. "Have you many signatures? And do you ever go around by yourself? Mr. Smallwood advised women to go around in couples."

"Mr. Smallwood," she snorted, "does not appreciate my worth. Why have two women going around where one will do? There were two of us to start with. But we thought we were wasting time, so we divided up our streets. We'll be able to do even more after we've completed the area assigned to us."

"My," I exclaimed. "You are an ardent Confederate, Mrs. Bloggs!"

"Nonsense," she replied. "I'm consistent, that's all. I always did say that Confederation should go on the ballot paper. That's not to say I'll vote for it, is it?"

"Maybe not," I admitted. "But you must see something in it or you wouldn't go to all this trouble."

"I like a square deal, Portia. That's reason enough for me."

"But you didn't tell me how you were getting on. I don't expect you got many signatures on this street."

"Portia, you invariably guess wrong," she retorted. "I've got many."

"But I'm sure Mrs. Haughty didn't sign. She's out-and-out for responsible government."

"Mrs. Haughty certainly did sign, after I got through with her," added Mrs. Bloggs with a grin.

"My goodness, Mrs. Bloggs. What kind of tactics are you using?"

"Logic, my child."

"Logic? What kind of logic?"

"Well, she said no, she couldn't possibly sign because she didn't agree with Confederation. She thought the terms were incomplete, though how she knows that is beyond me."

"And what did you say then?" I asked.

"Why I asked her if Confederation were on the ballot paper would she vote against it if the terms were incomplete, and she said she certainly would."

"And what did you say?"

"I gave her the same answer I had just given Mr. Average Citizen. He thought the issue was confusing."

"What did you say to him? Do tell me."

"I said, 'Look here Mr. Average. If Confederation was on the ballot would you vote against it if you thought anything about it was confusing?' He said he probably would."

"Go on, Mrs. Bloggs. I'm dying to hear what argument you used."

"Simple logic, my dear, simple logic. I just said to both of them, 'Well, how can you possibly vote against it unless it's on the ballot paper?'"

"Well, I'll be blowed!" I exclaimed. "And they both signed?"

"They did. Everybody did." She pushed her pen in my hand.

"Sign," she commanded.

I signed.

WOMAN OF THE WEEK

Over a three-year period, Dora's "Woman of the Week" provided readers with profiles of 140 local women. Dora was careful to draw on women from various walks of life. While many of them held occupations considered at the time "appropriate" for females, several of those profiled had broken through into careers previously reserved for men. The focus of this column was less overtly political with emphasis on individual achievements. The eclectic group selected for inclusion ranges from volunteers and nurses to business managers and a lawyer.

MRS. GRACE BUTT

Mrs. Grace Butt,[14] author and producer of the play *The Road through Melton* that met with appreciative audiences throughout its four-night run last week, sat one practice night at the back of the darkened hall. Punctuated by hammer blows and lighting experiments, she told of the work she had been doing.

"It was not just me," she assured me earnestly, "but every single member of the group. Of course, all members do not act. Many of them never look over the footlights. But they are just as essential to the production of a play as are the actors.

"Look at them now," she said, pointing to a few energetic workers. "Everyone doing his part. And there is

[14] Born in 1909, Grace Butt (nee Hue) was a founding member of the St. John's Players (1937), Newfoundland's first theatre company. In addition to *The Road through Melton*, she wrote several other plays as well as poems, short stories and documentaries. In 1981, Memorial University conferred on her an honorary degree (Doctor of Letters).

so much to do: carpentry, lighting, stage decoration, house management, music, makeup, costuming, business management, publicity. It is something of a business with its many and varied responsibilities all linking together for the good of the whole.

"We work hard," she admitted, "but we like it. We have done a little in the line of radio plays and hope to do more. Our aim is to build up a tradition through creative activity. We realize we have much to learn, as stage is entirely different from radio technique where the dramatic effect must be got by sound."

In speaking of the work of the St. John's Players, Mrs. Butt recalled the first play they produced nearly nine years ago, *The Admirable Crichton*. The group membership has changed since that time, she thought, but has also grown so that the outfit now numbers about forty members. The organization is anxious to enlist any newcomer who has dramatic leanings. Everybody is given the chance of reading for a part and the Casting Committee makes the final choice.

During the war, its funds went for patriotic purposes, and now with the purchase of a few necessities such as a carpet, a ceiling, lighting equipment and other incidentals, the group finds itself with little left to work on.

With regard to drama in Newfoundland, Mrs. Butt feels it has a future. "Get the people enthusiastic enough," she insists, "and small obstacles are soon overcome. A development of the arts in this country can do that.

"I don't say," she added, "that drama is more important than any other art, but it is naturally the liveliest of them. Linked with that is the fact that Newfoundland people have a strong sense of drama, because of the dramatic way in which we live.

"Why," she said, leaning forward earnestly as she spoke, "take the weather. Even the weather is dramatic in this country, when we consider the tragedies that take place every spring and fall.

"What we need," stated Mrs. Butt emphatically, "is a good stage, technical equipment and a workshop. I like to dream of a community building of the arts in St. John's in which might be housed not only a small but efficient theatre – a stage of our very own – but also the museum, an art gallery, and the Public Library. Such a building would be the centre of culture for the city.

"We can never be too grateful for the hospitality that the Memorial College has extended to us right from the beginning. Without this hospitality we might never have gone into action. If only somebody or some group would say. 'I like what you're trying to do. Here's a little theatre for you,' we could accomplish greater things in a shorter time."

ANNA TEMPLETON

Miss Anna Templeton,[15] who for the last six years has been organizing secretary of the Jubilee Guilds, sat in her newly decorated office in the Caribou Hut and invited admiration of the view of the harbour to be had from her window.

"We have been here for only three weeks," she said, "and we aren't properly settled. It's much nicer than

[15] The Anna Templeton Centre in St. John's reflects this woman's expertise and dedication. Opened in May 1994, the centre is committed to the advancement of craft, art and design throughout Newfoundland and Labrador.

were our quarters in the Brownrigg Building. We had only two little offices there, whereas here we have a large room for weaving classes besides a stock room and offices. It's a much nicer atmosphere, the surroundings are more cheerful and we feel we have room to move around. We hope to do good work here."

She outlined plans for the future: "We hope to give experimental and refresher courses now that we have more room. Our plan is to set up a series of classes in order to service the outports better. We feel that women could better learn weaving and other things we teach if we could take them in hand right here. Here we have the atmosphere of weaving and creative work, and the student absorbs more. Then, too, so many guild members come to St. John's at different times and would love to join our classes whilst they are in town.

"Both members and field workers work under great difficulties too. Sometimes it is hard to find a place to set up a loom, sometimes it is too cold at the meeting place to do good work, sometimes the women are detained at home with some household duty. These difficulties would be overcome to a certain extent if women could come to our classes for instruction. Not that it is our intention to discontinue the service we give in sending field workers out. Not by any means. But the classes would supplement the work we are doing in the field."

That the Jubilee Guilds are doing excellent work among the women of this country is evidenced by the fact that the branches are spreading so rapidly. There are now 107 guilds. The looms are locally made and there are 150 of them in use all over the country.

Speaking of the financial situation of the guilds Miss Templeton said, "We are almost independent. We get a grant from the government, but we have our own executive and we govern ourselves. It is important to feel independent, and to have women interested in the welfare of the other women in Newfoundland.

"We have made good progress during the last few years," she continued, "but it is essentially slow work. The art of weaving is ancient and it takes a long time to revive it."

As to the wisdom of attempting to revive an ancient and, in some opinions, an outworn art, Miss Templeton emphasized that the art was just as useful and worthwhile as hand knitting.

"We hope some day to make weaving available to the city folk, but our primary purpose is to encourage the art where it can do the most good - in the outports. That is where our work lies.

"Another thing we plan to do," she went on, "is to introduce more readable literature among the members. We need booklets written exclusively for Newfoundland, on canning, home produce, home decoration and so forth. To date we have been using mimeographed literature, but we feel that it does not make attractive reading, and that more members would be reached through the printed matter if it were properly published."

MISS NORA HOGAN

The capabilities of Miss Hogan[16] may be judged by the fact that she holds the position of manager for the

[16] Nora Hogan was the first woman to manage a movie theatre in St. John's. In fact, she managed two: the Paramount (on Harvey Road) and the Capitol (on Henry Street).

company which operates the Capitol and Paramount theatres.

"I've been in the theatre business for five years," she said, as we chatted in her comfortable office at the Paramount. "During that time I have worked at the Capitol theatre and at the Paramount since its opening in September 1944."

Prior to her career with the theatres, Miss Hogan studied music, attaining the degree of Liturgics and Church Music (LTCM), and gave lessons in pianoforte. To have the qualifications necessary to a career in music and in business is an unusual combination but Miss Hogan has the ability to work hard.

"There are so many odds and ends to attend to in a job of this sort that I don't think you could possibly be interested in them," she said. "However, I'll do my best to give you an idea of my work.

"I supervise a staff of about eighteen at each theatre, and pay their salaries – the projectionists, the ushers, assistants, cashiers, office girls, doormen, janitors. I greet the patrons in the lobby and try my best to give service and satisfaction. I have to settle many disputes, guard many valuable possessions, and look after the lost articles which are turned in and held until identified.

"Then I have to do the banking every day. Never yet have I missed a day, not even that exceptionally stormy Monday when the Water Street shops closed. I must be there, you see, to give in the day's receipts. It's the way we do business.

"My days and nights are both busy, and it is only on Sundays that I can relax at all. If I spend the morning at the Capitol theatre, I put in the afternoon at the

Paramount, and vice versa. I have to be around all the time, as I feel responsible for all that goes on.

"Our most difficult time was during the war, when we handled such huge crowds. Fortunately, we had a competent and reliable staff.

"Then, there is the office work. There are financial statements and returns to be made out, weekly reports to write, correspondence to deal with, and so on. I find plenty to do."

Miss Hogan works every day, including holidays, from 9 a.m. to 11 p.m. She feels she must be on the job constantly. As she expressed it, "slackness creeps in unless there is personal supervision."

DOROTHY MAUD VEY

Manageress of W. and G. Rendell, insurance and commission agents, is Miss Dorothy Vey,[17] who is proud of the fact that her firm, which represents the Phoenix Assurance Co. Ltd. of London, was the first insurance company office to operate in Newfoundland, being established in 1782.

A former student of Prince of Wales College, fellow schoolmates will remember her as prefect as well as captain of Pitts House for two years, where she was prominent in sports. Miss Vey took a commercial course and went with the firm of Job Bros., Insurance Department, where she worked for four years as stenographer. For the last six years, she has worked with the firm of W. and G. Rendell.

When in 1942 Mr. A.C. Rendell, owner of the firm, was suddenly afflicted with blindness which necessitated his

[17] A successful St. John's businesswoman, Dorothy Maud Vey was also a professional photographer and a keen bowler.

leaving the business temporarily, Miss Vey took over during his absence. "There was no one else to take over," Miss Vey explains simply. She carried on the worked so capably that she has ever since been Mr. Rendell's right hand, conducting the business with remarkable efficiency.

She carries a power of attorney from Mr. Rendell, whose comment is that she carries a heavy load of responsibility, and has done a good job.

Speaking of her work, Miss Vey says offhandedly, "I handled the finance and claims, bringing any particularly ticklish problems of a legal nature to Mr. Rendell. My work covers the filing of applications, issuing of policies, settlement of claims, all accounting to Head Office, as well as the supervision of half a dozen absentee landlord estates." She is also responsible for considerable amounts of money which she handles each year, and it is safe to assume that she holds one of the most responsible positions in the commercial life of St. John's.

The company's head office in Montreal also thinks highly of Miss Vey and has expressed its appreciation of her capabilities on more than one occasion.

Miss Vey also holds a diploma as a professional photographer, having completed a course with the New York Institute of Photography. "Sheer boredom," she laughs, "led me to take this seven months home study course. Photography is a fascinating study and makes a most absorbing hobby."

Also a keen bowler, Miss Vey is the daughter of organ builder W.I. Vey who has built church organs here, and who, in fact, is the most experienced man in the city capable of looking after church organs. Miss Vey may also be rated as an accomplished pianist – just another of the hobbies in which this remarkable woman excels.

NELLIE LUDLOW BRAND

Known and admired by thousands of lovers of swing music, Nellie Ludlow Brand[18] has made a name for herself in St. John's in the singing of popular songs.

One of our few professional songsters, the deep yet tender quality of her voice has that personal touch that puts her listeners "in the groove" as they shuffle and swing to the rhythm of Mickey Duggan's Orchestra.

"It started quite by accident, my singing," she explained. "When I was in Florida, a friend of mine who owned an exclusive restaurant asked me to sing there. She had a marvellous pianist, Ray Wilson. He could make that piano talk! He's playing now with the Blue Baroa Orchestra After that, I sang there often. Of course, that was definitely not professional work as far as I was concerned, but it was a beginning, and but for that invitation it would probably never have entered my mind to sing in public."

Better known by her maiden name, Nellie Ludlow sings regularly on Tuesday and Friday nights at the Old Colony Club, where her simple, girlish appeal has endeared her to her audiences. Her voice is a natural, and Nellie seems to know just what to do with it. She has been singing with Mickey Duggan's Orchestra for nearly two years now, and rates as our number one "torch" singer.

[18] Nellie Ludlow was a popular singer in St. John's, performing regularly with Mickey Duggan's Orchestra. Dora Russell was a fan. During the 1940s, she and her husband Ted spent many an evening at the Old Colony Club. Dora would occasionally be invited to play the piano.

The number of choruses she sings in an evening depends, she says, on the mood of the crowd. "Maybe I'll sing three numbers in a dance, maybe I won't sing one at all."

The songs that go over right now are "Wait and See," and "Personality," a present day hit made popular by Dorothy Lamour. "I enjoy specializing in slow numbers." Extremely fond of sentimental songs, her favourite is "Danny Boy," shared by millions of lovers of this ballad. A lover of classical music, she cherishes a secret desire to play the violin. "And I can't even play the piano," she mourns.

Many who attended the Playgrounds outdoor concert had the opportunity of hearing Nellie Ludlow for the first time and professed themselves delighted with her performance, given as it was under difficult singing conditions. She has been heard in broadcasts from the Old Colony Club and for a time was a radio announcer over VOCM. However, this work had to be given up, as the hours clashed with her singing time with the orchestra.

She finds the work very interesting. "I'm never bored," she says, "because I enjoy the contact with people."

Asked if she ever considers a more ambitious career in America, Nellie laughs, "Not me! I like it well enough right here. I was born here, and this is where I want to spend my life.

"It's been tough in many ways since I came home," she continues. "You see, I am seeking a divorce from my husband, and many people think a woman who is separated from her husband carries some sort of a stigma. I've had that to overcome."

Her marriage to an American at the age of sixteen did not work out well. Now a young girl of twenty-one, she is waiting for divorce proceedings to free her from an unfortunate union.

Nellie is a great lover of swimming and skating, enjoys trying out different strokes, and loves to dive. She likes to draw too. But most of all, she says, she "likes people."

MISS SYLVIA WIGH

The change from life in wartime England working with a naval commander at all kinds of secret jobs, to life in peacetime Newfoundland working with the Child Welfare Division of the Department of Public Health and Welfare may seem to be abrupt to many people. But to Miss Sylvia Wigh,[19] her present work, if not so exciting is just as interesting; and as for excitement, who wants too many big doses of it in one lifetime?

Miss Wigh's memories of her days during the war are very precious to her, but Newfoundland, her adopted country, means much to her; as soon as the war was over and it was feasible to come back, she came.

England is her birthplace but she came over here when she was very young, and all her family and most of her friends are here.

Shrewsbury in Shropshire is her home town and she began her education there. But her father, who is an antique dealer, came here for business reasons when she was very small. She continued her education at Bishop Spencer College, later going to Memorial. For a while

[19] Sylvia and Dora shared a close friendship, dating back to their years attending Bishop Spencer College. Later, Sylvia was active in the St. John's Players. A journalist, she was drama critic for several years with *The Evening Telegram*.

after graduating, she taught at Grand Falls and then at Bishop Feild but the war interrupted her work. She felt she had to go to London and see what she could do "to do her bit."

First of all she worked for the BBC, mainly on the program specially presented to South African listeners, and later on with the Allied Expeditionary Forces Program. Besides announcing, her time was spent helping the producers.

Then she got a job as social secretary to a young London socialite who had taken her children to the country away from the bombs. It was the husband of this lady who eventually became Sylvia's employer, and with him she took many trips to several of the beleaguered European countries. Most of these trips, Miss Wigh will tell you, and the means whereby the planes landed are still highly secret.

Her favourite and most amusing story of this period in her life concerns a trip to Holland. They fell in a ditch and had to hide out in a farmhouse. And they were soaking wet. The only covering the good lady of the house could provide while their clothes dried were horse blankets. And Miss Wigh says they could not get the smell of the stables off them for weeks.

When the war ended Miss Wigh took a well-deserved holiday in the south of France, and as she was the first visitor in the tiny village by the sea she was treated like a queen. The place had been the headquarters of a Luftwaffe Group and after this type of boarder the hotel keepers were only too glad to do all they could for the charming English lady. There was a special speech of welcome from the mayor and all the villagers who were mainly women children and old people. The young men had been killed by the Germans.

After this trip Miss Wigh joined a social service group of UNRRA[20] and was stationed for a time in Berlin. However, the strain of so much intense work with only a short holiday in between brought on a nervous breakdown and she came home to Newfoundland.

She is now an officer in Child Welfare, a job she loves, for it brings her in contact with people. People are sometimes amusing, sometimes maddening, but always interesting."

Her one hobby, and she is very earnest about it, is amateur dramatics. A hard-working member of the St. John's Players, she will be remembered for her performance as the young nurse, Sara, in Grace Butt's play commemorating the discovery of this country, *New Lands*. She is active in all phases of dramatics, and is as happy working on the set, making people up and collecting costumes, as she is acting. At the moment she is directing one of the Players' workshop plays entitled *Ladies in Retirement*.

MISS JESSIE B. MIFFLIN

The only person remaining of the six ladies who pioneered in Adult Education in 1932, Miss Jessie Mifflin, BA,[21] is now with the division of Visual Education, a branch of the Department of Education.

Miss Mifflin has gleaned an extensive knowledge of the country from her years as a field worker and adult

[20] The United Nations Relief and Rehabilitation Administration was an interim relief agency founded in 1943. It was absorbed into the United Nations in 1945.

[21] Jessie Mifflin grew up in Bonavista. After working for a while in Adult Education, she migrated in the 1940s to Visual Education, a division of the Department of Education. She was instrumental in helping build an extensive library of films. In the early 1960s she was a regular contributor to radio.

teacher. For the first four years of her connection with the Department of Education, she travelled all over the island, covering the north coast down to the Straits of Belle Isle, and along the south coast, spending two months in one settlement, two months in another. This experience has been invaluable to her in her present work. She then took over as acting field Secretary, and did this work for a year.

Miss Mifflin went to Columbia University in the summer months, where she took courses in Adult Education. The year of the Coronation,[22] she was given charge of the eight children who went to England to witness ceremonies and celebrations.

In 1942, Miss Mifflin severed temporarily her connection with Adult Education, when she was granted leave of absence to join the Air Force. During this time, she saw different parts of Canada, spending most of her time in Winnipeg. After a year, she was recalled to the Department to take over permanently the duties of field secretary.

When the work of the Department of Education was re-organized into rural and urban divisions, Miss Mifflin became the urban secretary, and helped in the organization and supervision of her districts. She continued with this work until last year, when the Film Board was taken over by the Department of Education, and Miss Mifflin was transferred there.

"The work is quite varied," Miss Mifflin explained. "I arrange programs for our nine field workers who travel the country, and I keep contact with them while they are out in the field, and arrange their itineraries. I plan

[22] King George VI, father of Queen Elizabeth II, was crowned in May 1937.

programs for the schools and clubs here in the city, and in addition, there are this year about twelve clergymen who own their own projectors. I arrange programs for them and send them out suitable films regularly. Several of the schools in urban areas have their own projectors (Corner Brook, Grand Falls, St. Michael's College and St. George's), and they get the same service. Then there are requests for films from Harmon Field, Argentia and Fort Pepperrell.

"There is never a dull moment with work of this type," Miss Mifflin declared. "We are kept very busy. Most of the city schools make use of our films. Where a school doesn't have its own projector, we send our men to give shows about four times a week. And we also send films to the Orthopaedic Hospital, the Mental Hospital, the Sanitarium, and although the latter hospital does not use many of our films, we provide the facilities. With the co-operation of Rotary Club, they obtain special films.

"Then we also cater to the Merchant Navy, the Handicraft centre, the Vocational Institute and the orphanages. A large number of church groups call for films, especially young people's societies, a few women's clubs and the YWCA. We give two or three shows every day of the week, all of which have to be properly planned and well balanced. An overdose of educational films is hardly the thing, so we include some entertainment in cartoons, singsong and sports films. At the present time, we get quite a demand for agricultural and co-operative films."

Miss Mifflin made it very clear that the work started by the Film Board has increased by leaps and bounds. "There is absolutely no comparison," she said, "between the work this year and last. Believe me, we don't spend our time just looking at films. We are kept very, very busy." Miss Mifflin herself has spent many of her half days and nights at work, cleaning up the jobs that could not receive her attention throughout the day. "But," she shrugs, "I like it so well, that it isn't work at all. It's a pleasure."

The Division of Visual Education has probably one of the largest library of films for the size of the country. Its 300 moving pictures are of every type and can meet the needs of all sorts of groups of people. Outsiders who view the collection with amazement declare that the library is better than any they have seen elsewhere. With such equipment at its disposal, it is no wonder that so much has been accomplished in the visual education field.

The machinery, unfortunately, is very expensive, and few schools other than the larger ones have been able to afford to buy their own projectors. Miss Mifflin feels that it is only a matter of time before schools all over the island will have them. Still pictures, however, are comparatively cheap, and many rural schools are showing these. A good library of filmstrips is being built up to serve these schools.

The projectionists cover the greater part of the island, except the Northern Peninsula, where travelling is difficult. Everywhere the films have been shown, they have been greatly appreciated, particularly in the smaller outports where films had never been seen. "It helps make the job interesting," Miss Mifflin said, "when you feel that you are making people happy while helping them."

There has been a constant demand for the five Newfoundland films that have been made, particularly from the bases, where so little is known of the country as a whole. Requests have even come in from Canada. One of the ten copies of *Silent Menace* has been placed in almost every district.

The combination of the Visual and Adult Education divisions is not actually complete as yet, although there is the closest co-operation between the workers. It is expected that when the contemplated change of quarters to Fort William has been made, the amalgamation will be complete.

MISS MONNIE G. MANSFIELD

Since 1929, the Newfoundland Memorial University has known, has felt and has benefitted from the presence on its staff of its registrar and Dean of Women, Miss Monnie G. Mansfield.[23]

Combining as it does the routine work of a registrar with the distinctly personal touch of a Dean of Women, the position which Miss Mansfield holds is unique in Newfoundland. Always able to call a student by name, Miss Mansfield holds that a college should give more than a mere academic education; it should preserve a personal contact with its students.

Upwards of 4,000 students have passed through the college since Miss Mansfield joined its staff, and "Monnie," as she is affectionately called, has been a mother to them all.

Now in its twenty-first year of life, the college has a students' registration this year of 431. These figures do not include the Teachers' Training enrollment.

[23] Monnie Mansfield joined Memorial University College in 1929 as college registrar and librarian. She retired in 1960 and was granted the honorary degree of Master of Arts.

"It was 111 when I first came here," recalls Miss Mansfield."The college opened in 1925, and I joined the staff four years later, as registrar and librarian.

"This," she continued, "is a real Newfoundland college. It is a cross-section of the whole country, as we have students here from all coasts, and from as far north as Indian Islands. In fact, there are always more outport than city students. Right now, we have 286 outport as against 195 city students.

"This raises one of our biggest problems - the need for a hostel to house the students.At present they are scattered all over the city, and sometimes the conditions under which they have to live are not conducive to good study."

Miss Mansfield's account of her work as registrar and Dean of Women leaves no doubt that it is far more than handling money and adding up figures.There is the constant contact with the students, which she loves, and the help which she gives them in their period of adjustment.

The jump from the supervised study of the school system and the method of teaching by lectures, when it rests with the student whether or not he will apply himself to his work, is such that a tremendous number of student problems are purely ones of adjustment. Students coming fresh from the schools are not prepared mentally for what they find in college.

All such difficulties, which are encountered in more or less degree by every college student, are smoothed over for the student by Miss Mansfield, who imposes upon herself the duty of keeping a non-academic as well as an academic attitude towards every student.

"It is important to get to know the students as quickly as possible," Miss Mansfield says. "They feel a great deal more at home if somebody is able to address them by their Christian names. Most of them are lonely. A number of them are shy. The fact that I'm not one of the teachers perhaps does something to win their confidence and makes them feel at home. Besides, they must learn more than facts if they are to acquire a true education. They must learn to live together, and you can't learn that in a classroom.

"I would like to see everybody with a college education. Here, we teach the students how to think. They have the benefit of meeting people from other parts of the island, and they gain from the inter-association of ideas. College life is good for this reason alone.

"Some of our students have done remarkably well," continued Miss Mansfield. "They have become teachers, lawyers, doctors, and have entered all sorts of professions and businesses. This college is not too big (and I hope it never will be) to see the problems of each individual.

"What makes the work worthwhile is the contact with youth. You have to be old enough to have good judgment, yet young enough to appreciate young people. The amount of development that can and does take place in a student in just two years is nothing short of marvellous."

Miss Mansfield began by teaching school, an experience which she has found valuable in her present work. She worked in a bank for a while, and then in a commercial office, but it was not until she found herself registrar of the Memorial University College that she felt she definitely belonged. From that day to this she has kept up her enthusiasm for her work. "If I hadn't," she remarked, "I couldn't have done it."

With regard to teachers, however, Miss Mansfield believes that the main thing is personality. "It gets things done," she asserts. "And then, there's the matter of approach. A teacher should be able to work with his pupils, and make them feel that he is one of them, and not somewhere high above them. Our job here is to turn out an all-round person and make him realize he has something to offer his country. He has, too."

Speaking of the late Professor J.L. Paton, past president of the college, Miss Mansfield said: "There was a man – a great man. I think we all imbibed a little of his spirit. He made everybody try to be better than they actually were, because he always believed the best of them himself. They tried to live up to his estimate of them. Doing the job wasn't good enough for Mr. Paton, unless you gave something of yourself, unless you were influenced by the desire to give service."

Everybody has a latent something to be developed, believes Miss Mansfield. Everybody, she thinks, has his proper niche in life to fill, if he can find it. She likes to help him find it, for, as she says, "The greatest tragedy in life is to find round people trying to fit themselves into square holes."

MISS STELLA BURRY

Miss Stella Burry,[24] deaconess of the United Church in Newfoundland, was born in Greenspond. She later taught school in Port Nelson, George's Brook and Curling. She then entered the United Church Training School

[24] A deaconess and pioneer social worker, Stella Burry founded Emmanuel House, providing food, shelter and counselling to those in need. "Stella's Circle" (on Rawlins Cross in St. John's) is her legacy.

in Toronto, where she took a two year course to fit her work as deaconess.

We interviewed Miss Burry in the big empty rooms of the building on the corner of Cochrane Street and Military Road, which is to be opened as the new Community Centre the second week in June. Perched upon a radiator, we heard the story of her work and her hopes for the future.

Miss Burry began her work with Rev. Peter Bryce in East Toronto, a new district which was opening up at that time, and in which a great many old country people were settling. She spent four years at this work, and then the call came to go to downtown Toronto.

There, at the Carlton St. Church called the Hall of Friendship, Miss Burry worked as Deaconess among great numbers of young people and strangers. Minister of the church was Rev. E.C. Hunter, son of the evangelist.

"We served a great many needy people during the Depression," Miss Burry said. "The church acted as a counselling centre. Streams of young people - and older folks too - came to us for comfort and advice. In those days of the Depression there were so many frustrated people. We did a lot of personal work during the ten years I spent there."

About that time, due to the efforts of Rev. Oliver Jackson, who felt that social work in the United Church should be organized, an opportunity was opening up in this country for a social worker, and Miss Burry was appointed to the position. She began work here in September 1938. Rooms were opened up at Adelaide and New Gower streets.

"In the first days we were very busy, acting as a relief centre and visiting the needy among our people. As time went on, however, we felt the need of a place for girls and women, where they could find fellowship and recreation."

The rooms soon developed into a community centre, which interested its members in health, nutrition, cooking and sewing.

A small buying club was organized, and it was a familiar sight to find women dropping in with their baskets to buy from the forty-seven varieties the centre offered. This buying club developed into a credit union which is still operating, and which incidentally, is the only known women's co-operative credit union in the country.

"Another great need was filled," continued Miss Burry, "when we began to cater to the young girls working in homes. One year we had so many that we had to divide into two groups. More than one girl remarked, 'When I step inside the door, I feel that I am home.'

"The first year we were in operation we helped 275 children go to school. We held summer schools for the underprivileged, which were a combination of Christian teaching, recreation and cultural education. We also had the fun of setting up a summer school in the old camp tradition at the Jackson-Walsh Memorial Camp, Western Bay. Dedicated to the memory of Rev. Jackson, the camp has been running for four years."

January 28 was a disastrous date for the Community Centre, for on that day, the Star Building was gutted by fire and the centre lost everything it had worked so hard to gain - everything but the spirit of its members, who continued to hold together despite obstacles.

"Things looked pretty black," admitted Miss Burry, "but we immediately began to plan for the future, and now that we have acquired this lovely building it seems too wonderful to be true. It fits our needs so perfectly. We owe a great deal to the small group of businessmen who, when the building was for sale, seized the opportunity to acquire it for the church.

"It is most conveniently fixed for our work. We plan to use the ground floor and basement space for our office and group work. The other two floors are ideal for the work I have always felt needed attention – a residence for young outport girls in the lower income bracket who come to the city to work. I feel that mothers in outports would be happy to know there was such a place for their girls. I hope someday to be able to set up a training centre for young girls who work in homes and help them find positions. I hope to see a registry set up for young girls who come to town, so as to be able to extend the friendship of the church in a more personal way. City girls will use the centre too, as a place where they can relax and find recreation. I hope it may become a home for many young girls, where they may receive the friendship and counsel of the church.

"During my eight years working here, I have been greatly concerned over the waste of womanhood. Service for young women is one of the focal points in church social work, and we do hope that the centre will be widely used by all our church people."

DR. FLORENCE O'NEILL

Dr. Florence O'Neill,[25] now assistant director of Adult Education, received her early education at the

[25] Florence O'Neill dedicated her working life to Adult Education. In 1944, she became the first person in what is now Canada to earn a doctoral degree in that field. After twelve years as director in Newfoundland, she moved to Ottawa to organize Adult Education for the Department of Indian Affairs.

Presentation Convent, Witless Bay, where she was born. Graduating from high school at an early age, she began her work in that field in which she was destined to make her career. For six years she taught in various outport schools. It may be significant that she too made her beginning where the late Lord Morris began his career, on the island of Oderin.

"From my earliest childhood," said Dr. O'Neill, "I had an insatiable thirst for knowledge. My love of people in all walks of life prompted my desire to acquire the necessary information and to utilize it in the best interests of my country.

"Oh, but the road was not easy," she said. "During my undergraduate years I never had the opportunity of doing two consecutive years at college, but by alternating two years teaching and one year college, by saving, working summers with the Playground Association, marking papers and doing all sorts of odd jobs, my dreams of graduation were finally realized."

Dr. O'Neill graduated from Dalhousie University in 1936 with a BA in Education. However, before taking her final year, that same interest in humanity prompted the desire to learn something of the unpleasant side of city life. Accordingly, she became the first woman stenographer of the Central District Court, having previously worked up a business course on her own. Adult classes held at night for a small group of advanced pupils contributed to her ultimate ambition.

On graduation from Dalhousie, Dr. O'Neill joined the Adult Education staff here and by special request was sent to some of the most isolated sections of the country. She continued this work for six years. Concerning her work during this period she says, "I would not have missed this opportunity for the world. It has given me invaluable information, appreciation of people generally, a deeper understanding of their way of life and a background of experience, otherwise impossible to acquire. Furthermore it has confirmed my faith in Adult Education as an important factor in promoting positive social change."

Dr. O'Neill, having convinced herself of the importance of Adult Education on a much broader basis, attended a summer school at Columbia University, New York, in 1939 which only whetted her appetite. She says, "I was still hungry for the opportunity to do uninterrupted study and so in 1942, I returned to Columbia to do further work towards my master's degree." The longed-for opportunity eventually arrived. Dr. O'Neill enjoyed the distinction of being offered a Carnegie Fellowship as well as a Rockefeller Fellowship and three Dean Scholarships from Columbia University.

"This made it possible for me to study for my doctor's degree," continued Dr. O'Neill, "and at this point, I may say I could hardly believe that my goal was in sight. It was my first really lucky break.

"The work was hard," Dr. O'Neill admitted, "and it was one continual grind, working through summer school and intersessions, but there was always the incentive of having a great hope realized. During my studies I met many stimulating people. Life at International House was exciting. I met the greater part of 550 students, representing fifty-seven different nationalities. This was an education in itself. I was the only Newfoundlander."

During her final year at Columbia, much of her time was devoted to outside activities as well as work of a professional nature.

She was assistant to the head of the Department of Adult Education at Teachers College, president of the Adult Education Club, member of the student council at both Teachers College and International House and was elected to Kappa Delta Pi and Pi Lambda Theta, national honorary fraternities. As the guest of Wisconsin University, Dr. O'Neill did field work in Adult Education. She was the recipient of an honorarium which made it possible for her, over a period of five weeks, to travel in seven countries, address mixed groups and see Adult Education in action in that most prosperous state of Wisconsin.

Finally, Dr. O'Neill received her degree of doctor of education and has the distinction of being the only Newfoundland woman to obtain a doctor's degree in education from Columbia University, New York.

After graduation Dr. O'Neill was offered many lucrative positions in the United States, but she preferred to return to her native Newfoundland and even after returning, has declined several most promising and tempting appointments.

Since the autumn of 1944 she has worked as assistant director of the Division of Adult Education and has made a valiant effort to inaugurate a re-organized program.

"I still feel that the project we have been trying to put across is the answer to a long-felt need in Newfoundland," she said earnestly. "While it is not a panacea for all our ills, it can do much to bring about social change in this country of ours. It is designed to train leaders and to help people to help themselves, a most important factor in the rehabilitation and reconstruction of our country."

MARGARET F. GODDEN

"It's the nicest job in town," asserts Margaret F. Godden,[26] speaking of her work as secretary in the Tourist Bureau office.

Miss Godden was secretary of the Tourist Board for a number of years, until it resigned in a body last December as a result of the government's rejection of its tourist plans. The Tourist Board no longer exists, but the bureau still pursues its multitudinous tasks, with Miss Godden's capable fingers feeling its pulse.

Miss Godden is a familiar figure in many of the tourist offices away, and declares that in this country "we have the nicest setup of any." She spent six weeks last spring doing contact work in New York and New Jersey and visited offices in Vermont and Connecticut, where she made herself known, saw for herself what was being done there, "and," she added, "took care of any tourists they wanted to send to Newfoundland."

Her work is varied and interesting. "We take care of all inquiries that come in," she said, "plan trips for people, choose rivers for them, get accommodation, guides, boats, food, licenses, arrange transportation if needed, make train reservations, help them decide whether or not they want a cruise in a coastal boat, take care of hunting parties, arrange sightseeing tours, and usually keep contact with them until they have left the country. We buy anything they want, which is a service

[26] Margaret Godden was secretary of the Tourist Bureau. She undertook several initiatives that helped put Newfoundland on the map for potential visitors. Her favourite hobby was fishing.

you don't find elsewhere. Of course, other bureaus work on a percentage basis whereas we do not take money for anything. The government finances us."

As Miss Godden pointed out, the service was built up from nothing. "We didn't know where to turn for information when we first started," she said, "but we found everybody we approached most willing to help. We get information from the clergy, the rangers and the police, the department, the river wardens. Now we have a set of files built up that are of immense help to us."

It would be quite natural to assume that the winter months should find the Tourist office experiencing a slack time. Miss Godden laughed at our suggestion that this was so. "I worked four nights a week and Sundays," she pointed out, "from December to May, answering enquiries, and that, at a time when we were doing no advertising. We haven't advertised you know, since the war. Since the beginning of the year, we have handled over 2000 letters, and that with a staff of only one girl to help."

Asked if many enquiries came to anything, Miss Godden replied that the percentage was difficult to ascertain. So many parties, after making enquiries, proceeded on their trip with no further contact with the office. She believed, however, that the percentage of enquiries resulting in tourist trips was very high indeed in comparison with that of other bureaus.

"And," she continued, "they must be satisfied, because we find even with poor accommodation and sometimes poor fishing conditions the same people are coming again and again. We have to turn down a number of people, but we try to fit them in another time. We haven't the accommodation available to handle them all."

During the war, when the tourist business was very slack indeed, the bureau busied itself providing hospitality for officers, obtaining houses for servicemen and their families, handling as many as 1,700 requests for houses. In all, some 20,000 servicemen received attention from the Tourist Bureau.

Miss Godden is familiar with nearly all the fishing rivers in the country, and tries each year to visit some new place, so that she is in a position to advise from personal experience. An ardent fisherman herself, she has cast a line in most of the rivers in the country. She knows the average size of the fish that can be taken and the best time of the season, which varies at different rivers, and if prospects of a good fishing trip are poor, she makes an honest reply to the enquiring tourist, who usually responds to this unusual treatment by making the trip another year.

MISS ELIZABETH ANGEL

The week of October 6-11 will be Junior Red Cross week all over Newfoundland. In this connection, we asked Miss Elizabeth Angel,[27] who is the organizer of the Junior Red Cross in Newfoundland, with the Department of Public Health and Welfare, to give us some information as to the object and aim of this special week.

Junior Red Cross, said Miss Angel, has three primary aims. First, and most important of course, is to make the children of Newfoundland "health conscious"; in other words, encourage them to acquire clean sanitary personal habits, which, if practiced as children, will follow

[27] A nurse by profession, Elizabeth Angel worked with the Department of Public Health and Welfare during the Commission of Government. She was organizer of the Junior Red Cross.

them all through life, and make better citizens of them in years to come. Secondary, to teach children to be good citizens and encourage them to think for themselves. When Junior Red Cross groups are formed, they hold their meetings in accordance with Parliamentary procedure, hold discussions and debates, and are encouraged to express their own opinions. Thirdly, as there are branches of Junior Red Cross all over the world this organization helps to promote international friendships, which is interesting as well as educational; in no better way can good citizenship and international friendship be promoted than through the children of different countries, with the common ideal of service to others.

For this particular week in October, Junior Red Cross is working in close co-operation with the Newfoundland Tuberculosis Association. Both of these organizations feel that making children "health conscious," encouraging and teaching them to eat the proper foods and acquire proper hygiene habits while they are young, will be a good step forward in years to come in the prevention of that dread menace, tuberculosis. Junior Red Cross is going to appeal to every boy and girl all over the country to buy the red double-barred cross, which is the emblem of the TB Association, and ask them to do everything they can to help in the fight against this disease.

Members of the Junior Red Cross perform in their small way a surprising number of services all the year round. For instance, children from all over the country, even in very remote settlements, send in homemade quilts, little knitted suits, sweaters and toys, made by the children to help the poor and needy. Children of the Red

Cross raise funds every year to send a deaf mute to school in Halifax, and hope to help out crippled children too. They visit hospitals and bring little gifts to the sick – last year some of the girls volunteered to help out as nurses' aides at the Grace Hospital in the Children's Ward. The Junior Red Cross is now planning to send large plaques of nursery rhymes, particularly Mother Goose, to all the hospitals in the city, to help brighten up the hours for the sick kiddies.

Junior Red Cross are featuring window displays to sponsor their week in which members will take part, and the children will change places every hour. There will also be a radio program, which will no doubt be very interesting and entertaining, to help make people see the objects and aims of the organization.

There are at present 1,000 branches of the Junior Red Cross all over the country, and 31,000 members. It is now in its twelfth year in Newfoundland. Miss Angel would particularly like to see more high school pupils join. "Girls and boys of the teenage group could do marvelous work," she said. "If they formed their own councils to plan and carry out their own ideas, they could look after the younger children, and supervise the sponsoring of different kinds of health weeks."

Miss Angel finds her work so very interesting, it is difficult to persuade her to bring a personal note into the conversation. When asked how she happened to take up this particular kind of work she replied, "In preliminary training with the department, we have a week of Junior Red Cross, and this work appealed to me very much." In the course of her duties, keeping personal contact is very important; last year she visited branches on Bell Island, Trinity South, Bonavista North, the Green Bay area, and was flown by Aero Sales and Service to the St. Anthony district, travelled as far as Reef's Harbour and also visited Southern Labrador and Norris Point. "In all the places visited," she said, "people were very kind and friendly, and I enjoyed meeting them very much."

Miss Angel and members of the staff are working very hard to make Junior Red Cross week a big success, and it is sincerely hoped that many people in the country will see the amount of good this organization is really doing to make the next generation of Newfoundlanders better citizens and healthier than ever before.

MISS MARGARET GUY

This week the Macdonald Fellowship Club held their annual dinner and as is usual at these affairs the officers changed over. Normally "Woman of the Week," when noting occasions such as these, casts its light on one of the newly selected officers, but this week for a change we are reversing the procedure and momentarily stopping one of the retiring officers in her trip out of office.

Miss Margaret Guy[28] for the past year has very efficiently carried out the exacting duties of secretary of the club which is the senior branch of the Young Women's Christian Association.

During her term in office the Macdonald Fellowship Club has had a very full year, mingling entertainment

[28] Margaret Guy served as a field worker for Adult Education. She is best remembered as one of the pillars of the teaching staff at Prince of Wales College in St. John's. (On a personal note, Miss Guy was my Grade Eleven home-room teacher in 1954-55.)

with the more serious side of things. At the suggestion of the Child Welfare Department the club undertook to help ten foster children living in the vicinity of Manuels. Later on the number of children was increased to fourteen.

Miss Guy and other members of the club made periodic visits to these children to ascertain their needs and to meet them. They held two jumble sales and two card parties. Out of the money realized the club supplied the children with needed clothing, gave them a much enjoyed summer picnic and played Santa Claus at Christmas.

Also during Miss Guy's term of office the club gave a substantial amount to the Oslo fund and recently passed over a large cheque to the YWCA. This money was raised by card parties and other schemes, all of which simply piled the work on Miss Guy's capable shoulders.

Born in Carbonear several years ago, Margaret Guy is now a teacher at Prince of Wales College, but before joining the staff there she was a field worker with Adult Education. During her career with this branch of the department she travelled just about all over Newfoundland spending no more than two months in each place. All in that short space of time she had to organize home study groups, youth clubs, and teach a class the fundamentals of the three R's.

At the Adult Education night schools everyone over sixteen was made quite welcome, although the wider the range of pupils the more difficult Miss Guy's work became. She found that the classes were very popular and the people flocked to them in droves. As time was limited it was found that Miss Guy could only give her eager pupils the basic rules of reading 'riting and 'rithmetic, but once given this base, the students would proceed on their own with their teacher visiting them from year to year as often as the pupils wanted her, correcting mistakes and giving still further knowledge with each visit.

Miss Guy's most vivid memory of these days is a picture of an old lady who was extremely keen to learn. Having given the groundwork, the teacher had to leave; but on her return the next year she found that the old lady had continued her studies on her own, and had progressed so far that she could now pick up a book and read it without difficulty. A year earlier the old lady did not even know the alphabet. Now her greatest thrill was to get and answer a letter.

Acting as the Macdonald Fellowship Club Secretary, all Miss Guy's spare time recently has been taken up in organizing the annual dinner held last Wednesday night at the Newfoundland Hotel. Fortunately for her peace of mind, the genial hotel manager took complete control of all actual dinner menus, seating arrangements, etc. Otherwise Margaret would have been overwhelmed by the rush of details connected with preparing for a club dinner.

Now all the extra work is over, Miss Guy can relax a little and catch up with her reading.

MISS LOUISE SAUNDERS

Evidently, in 1910, there was some doubt whether the word "person" included a woman, because on March 22 of that year, the Newfoundland Legislature passed an Act amending the Law Society Acts so that where in that

Act the word "person" occurred, that word should be held to extend to and include women.

This most far-sighted action on the part of the legislature brought to the fore, in later years, Newfoundland's first woman lawyer, Miss Louise Saunders,[29] who, by dint of hard work and many hours of intense study, succeeded eventually in mastering the technicalities of law.

"Of course," she says cheerfully, "one is always studying. Law is like that. There is always more to learn."

Miss Saunders has been practicing law since 1933. She defines law as "the rules which we have formed for getting along with one another peaceably to negate the doctrine that 'Might is Right,' and the lawyer is the person who has learnt these rules and is therefore able to act as guide to others. No lawyer can know all the complicated niceties of all rules, but he knows where to find them and must be continually studying."

The routine of daily work in a lawyer's office includes "everything that comes," as Miss Saunders laughingly puts it. That means such things as probates, administration of estates, transfer of property, collection work, workmen's compensation, property rights, making of wills, notarial work.

"Speaking of practice," Miss Saunders said, "one Newfoundland lawyer was employed by a corporation and was not doing work other than that of the corporation. He was approached by a man who wanted to take out a summons. He replied that he could not do that because he was not in practice. The man answered that

[29] Born in Greenspond, Louise Saunders was Newfoundland's first woman lawyer. She was called to the bar in 1933, and began her career as legal secretary for, and later partner of, the former prime minister, Richard Squires.

oh, it was only a small thing, he wouldn't need much practice to handle that!"

Miss Saunders has some advice to give ladies on making statements in court.

"To get the truth," she says, "a witness is allowed only to state the truth, the whole truth and nothing but the truth. It is useless to say, 'Oh yes, I know she was there, Mom told me.' That would be squashed immediately. So, ladies, no gossip will get you by in court.

"However," she continued, "the good lawyer's idea is to keep his client out of court if possible. And from that purpose we have all the Whereases, Wherefores and Saids and other language in documents which may be regarded as archaic or quaint. As in every other profession and trade, certain expressions are 'symbols' of a great deal. Certain words and expressions have come during the centuries to mean a whole series of ideas.

"In the preparation of wills, there is necessity for the exercise of imagination. Unless it is a very simple will, the lawyer must visualize what will happen to his client's property perhaps twenty-five or thirty years hence, and must make sure that the true intention of his client is expressed in language that will be absolutely unambiguous.

"The lawyer is one who knows his way around with regard to the relation of people one with the other, one whose duty is to protect his client at all times and to see him safely through the inevitable mazes connected with the complicated rights and duties of everyday living.

"In this, the Newfoundland lawyer has a high standard of professional honour and courtesy. When this country was settled, the English law applied, and has from time to time been modified and altered to suit local conditions.The Newfoundland Bar upholds the great traditions of English jurisprudence.

"The legal profession is one to which patience, perseverance and probity must be brought. In return the lawyer has work which is never monotonous. It brings him in direct contact with people and their problems. It is an extremely interesting work, for problems are brought to you every day and the encouraging part about it is that you can usually do something about them.

"I have used the word 'he' in speaking of a lawyer," Miss Saunders concluded with a smile, "but in analogy to the Law Society Act, words importing men include women."

We should think so!

DAY BY DAY

Dora wrote over 200 of these entries during a two-year period (1946-48). A fictional diary, "Day by Day" follows a typical St. John's family as it deals with daily domestic concerns. In this respect, it is quite different from the political columns. The family comprises a father, mother and three children (with a fourth coming along in due course). Much of the material was gleaned from Dora's own experiences as a wife and mother, with one notable difference: the mother in "Day by Day" is a "stay-at-home mom" while Dora - though married with four children - most certainly was not.

In 1983, Dora selected a series of entries covering the year 1946 and published them as Day by Day: Pages in the Diary of a Newfoundland Woman *(Harry Cuff Publications).*

January 1, 1946

Here's how things are at our house.

My name is Mary Smith and I'll soon be forty. My husband, John, works with the Department of Finance as an accountant.

We have three children. There's Linda Mae. She's ten and quite a grown-up young lady. Or at least she has grown-up ideas. Despite this, however, here she is now, stretched out on the floor pretending she is lying in bed, with Judy's doll in her arms.

Judy, the youngest of the family, is five years old. She is bawling at the top of her voice. She has a slide. She has a dustpan and mop. She has blocks and balloons and goodness knows what else. But she wants only one thing now. Her doll.

The remaining member of the family is Daphne. She'll soon be eight. We call her Daffy. When you get to know her, you'll understand why. The name just comes naturally to us, because she is the mischief maker in this family. She should have been born a boy, for she gives such a good imitation of one that I have never really been sorry that our family did not include a boy.

Linda, Daphne and Judy do not agree. They want a new baby. Not me. Three is enough.

Right now, Daffy is abnormally quiet. The reason is that she is up in my room putting lipstick on her face. Ordinarily Linda would be the culprit, but today Linda has forgotten her lady-like impulses and remembers only that she is a little girl who didn't get a doll for Christmas.

When I shoo Daffy from my room, I shall find her later going about with her feet in her father's slippers. Then John will grumble, "I can't see why you don't keep the children from getting at my things. Don't they have anything to play with?"

And that's our family. Except me. Me, I'm just an ordinary harassed housewife with three children underfoot, a budget that has to be stretched to meet rising costs, and more work to do than I can find time for.

Just like any other mother.

January 2

John awoke this morning and looked at the brilliant sunshine. "A new year!" he exulted. "You know, Mary, there's something about starting a new year. I'm going to begin on the right foot. I'm going to jump out of bed now and get to the office early. There's plenty of work there waiting for a good, energetic man to do, and I'm the man to do it."

With these brave words he jumped out of bed. I groaned, as that meant I had to jump too. I wished his New Year's resolutions would include getting himself off to work, complete with breakfast, rubber footwear and handkerchief.

Still brisk and energetic, John put on his overcoat and prepared to leave for work.

"Mary," he asked, "where's my hat?"

"Goodness, I don't know where your hat is, John. Don't you usually hang it with your coat?"

"Yes, but it's not there now. Look for yourself. There isn't a hat in sight."

I looked. Right enough, there wasn't a hat in sight, unless you count my new black number with the scarlet feather.

"I must have left it somewhere New Year's Eve," said John as he bent to find his gaiters.

He straightened himself. "Mary, where are my gaiters? They're not here."

"Oh John, they must be there. Where else could they be?"

But they weren't there. That was very evident.

"I guess you must have left them somewhere too," I ventured.

"I guess I did," he said sheepishly. "Well, what am I going to do now? I can't go out in this slippery weather without gaiters."

I looked at the clock. "Well, you're late for work anyway," I said. "So you might as well be later. Better go downtown and get something to put on your feet."

So John, considerably chastened, picked his way carefully over to the nearest bus stop and went off downtown.

January 3

"Mommy," said Linda pensively. "Is it too late to make New Year's resolutions?"

"What's revolutions?" asked Judy.

"Well, it's like you make up your mind to be good or do something for somebody every day."

"Of course it's not too late," I assured Linda. "It's still time to make them."

"Well, I'm going to make one. I'm going to work for you one day, Mommy, and the next I'm going to do Daffy's work for her, and the next I'll do Judy's - and like that every day."

I saw Daffy's eyes brighten. "I got the taps to shine this week," she remarked.

"Well," replied Linda, "I'll start today and do Daffy's work."

"I got the washbowl to clean, too," Daffy chirped in.

"OK, I'll shine the taps and clean the wash bowl."

"And I got to polish the piano."

"Oh," said Linda, a bit dispirited but soon brightening with determination. "I'll do that, too. Where's the cloth?"

And she set to work with a will. An hour later, she sank into a chair.

"All done?" I asked her.

"Yes, Mommy."

"Doesn't it make you feel good, doing something for someone else?" I ventured.

Linda hesitated. "Yes," she said with a doubtful sigh. "But I think I need a rest, so tomorrow I'll just work for myself."

Which I personally considered a very wise resolution.

January 5

Linda and Daphne just don't seem to get along as well as I should like them to. They are entirely different in both outlook and character, so I suppose that accounts for it.

Linda is, first and foremost, a lady. She yearns to be grown up. She is tidy and fastidious and watches older people for reactions and behaviour so that she will know how to act herself. Daffy shocks her continually with her forthrightness and lack of tact. Linda cannot understand such behaviour at all, and Daffy is scornful of Linda's reactions, accusing her of trying to act "proud."

As they are so utterly different in temperament, I suppose it is quite natural that they should fail to see eye to eye on many things. In fact, they quibble over the silliest things.

Today it was over Winston Churchill!

How they got on the subject of Churchill as a surname I don't recall, as I was not paying attention to them. But I did hear Daffy ask, "How do you know there is anyone by the name of Churchill?"

"There's a girl in our Sunday School class by the name of Churchill," Linda stated.

"How do you know?" retorted Daffy. "Did her mother tell you her name is Churchill? She might be pretending."

"Well then," said Linda defensively, "there's a man who works at *The Evening Telegram* and his name is Churchill."

"How do you know?" insisted Daffy. "Did he say his name was Churchill?"

"Well no," admitted Linda, "he didn't say, but everyone calls him Mr. Churchill - so his name must be Churchill."

"That might be a nickname," persisted Daffy. "Lots of people got nicknames, but nicknames are not surnames."

"Well then," said Linda in exasperation, "there's Winston Churchill. He's a Churchill!"

Daffy snorted, as only Daffy can. "You don't know that either."

"Go on!" cried Linda. "Everybody knows Mr. Winston Churchill in the war. His picture was all over everywhere. Now you can't say there was no Mr. Churchill."

"I can too," retorted Daffy. "How do you know? Did you ever ask him if his name was Churchill? Did he ever *tell* you?"

At this point I had to intervene as the argument was rapidly growing heated. "Daffy," I reprimanded, "it is a grand thing to know all the facts, but there are so many facts in the world that we have to take somebody's word for it that most of them can be believed. Now people believe that there is a Winston Churchill, and if you are a wise little girl you will accept that all the people in the world cannot be wrong."

And Daffy subsided. Unwillingly.

January 8

"I'm going to enjoy a nice quiet evening," said John firmly. "I'm going to take off my shoes and smoke my last Christmas cigar while listening to soft music. If I fall asleep in my armchair, you can lead me gently to bed."

"As bad as that?" I asked in surprise. "Did you have a strenuous day at the office?"

"I did," said John. "In fact, I have had a succession of strenuous days. And nights. How you women stand up to this Christmas racket is more than I can understand."

"Nonsense," I said. "Trouble with you is that you are getting old."

"Trouble with you," he retorted, "is that you think you're younger than you are. What's wrong with home, anyway? And what's wrong with staying in it once in a while?"

I didn't bother to argue the point. John is out of the house every day. He doesn't understand what it is to be stuck in the same old place, all day and all night too.

John dropped onto the chesterfield and closed his eyes.

"Keep the children out of here," he demanded.

I did my best, but you can't keep track of three children all at the one time, and they are so forgetful.

Linda wandered into the room. "Mommy, what's wrong with Daddy? What's he got his eyes closed for? Daddy, why are your eyes closed?"

"Go away," said John sleepily.

Then I lost track of Judy. She had made for the living room. I hurried to get her out of it, but not in time. She was tapping John on the forehead.

"Look what I did," she said with a triumphant smile, waving a piece of paper in front of John's eyes. "Look, Daddy. That's a little girl - see - and that's where she's holding her balloons. Daddy, can I have a balloon off the tree?"

"Go away," said John wearily.

"But Daddy, you didn't look."

"Go away," said John, raising his voice.

Judy fled.

Then Daffy went in to get Judy's doll from under the tree. Judy won't go anywhere without her doll. And Judy was afraid to go into the room to get it. Daffy tripped over the doll's carriage and let out a howl.

"Go away," shouted John. Then he got up and reached for his shoes.

"Where are you going? I asked.

"I'm going out," he grunted. "For a rest."

And he stamped out of the house.

January 21

The touch of winter was nice while it lasted. The children dragged out their coasters and off they went. After a while, Linda came in to complain that the steering gear on hers wouldn't work.

"Here, I'll fix it," offered John.

Well, maybe he tried to fix it but not so that it could work. John's 'fixing' usually ends up that way.

"I'd better take it out and try it," he offered, as he stood and looked at the job.

So John trudged to the top of the street, dragging the slide behind him, and proceeded to try it out.

Linda waited patiently. Time slipped by.

John was on his seventh run when Linda came back into the house. "Mommy," she fretted, "it's taking Daddy a long time to see if the steering works alright."

"It is," I agreed, "but perhaps he is enjoying the sliding himself."

"Well, why don't he take turns on all the slides?" she complained.

"You've got something there," I said, and called out to John.

He came over. "It's getting to work fine now," he announced, "but I think I'd better have a few more runs just to make sure."

"But I want to slide," wailed Linda.

So Linda Mae took her coaster and began to slide, with John watching her.

But not for long. A few minutes later I looked out the window and, not altogether to my surprise, I saw John on Daffy's slide, while she waited patiently by the side of the road.

January 25

I took Daphne to church this morning.

Daffy likes very much to sing. If she knows the hymns she will join in them wholeheartedly. If she doesn't, she will join in them just the same!

The congregation began singing a hymn. Daffy didn't know it very well. Caught up by the singing, she joined in with the first tune that came to her head.

"She'll be comin' round the mountain when she comes," she sang in jubilant triumph. "She'll be comin' round the mountain when she comes." I threw her a warning look but it was too late.

The hymn ended with a reverend "Amen." Daffy's voice, still lifted in song, began to trail off, though still conspicuous: "She'll be comin' round the mountain when she comes."

It is fortunate for my peace of mind that I have a sense of humour. Sometimes, anyway. Apparently, the people sitting nearby enjoyed the whole thing, for an audible titter followed.

For a moment the solemnity of the service was disrupted. But it soon was restored. I felt like pretending this was not my child, but since we were the only ones in the pew I knew I would not get away with it.

I determined to have a heart to heart talk with Daffy after church.

FEATURE ARTICLES

In addition to her busy schedule preparing the columns for "A Page for Women," Dora Russell was The Evening Telegram *staff reporter who covered the daily proceedings of the National Convention. She was also assigned articles on topics of general interest, two of which appear below. The second is on a subject literally close to home. Churchill Park, referred to locally as "the Housing," was a subdivision of St. John's, built in the area immediately north of Empire Avenue and both east and west of Allandale Road. In early 1946 the first homes went on sale. One of the first to move in (during July) was the Russell family - Dora, Ted and their four young daughters.*

BOWRING PARK: A SOURCE OF PLEASURE (1946)

Hundreds of citizens throng Bowring Park on Sundays and holidays, a happy testimony to the munificence of the firm of Bowring Brothers both here and in other parts of the world. It celebrated its centenary in 1911 with a gift to the public of Newfoundland of Bowring Park.

Set in the beautiful Waterford Valley, the park, formerly the Rae Island Farm and the property of Miss Neville, was purchased through Sir Edgar Bowring. The laying out of the park was begun in 1911. Plans were made by Frederick G. Todd, a well-known landscape architect from Montreal, whose designs were carried out by the late M.R.H.K. Cochius, a landscape artist in his own right.

On July 14, 1914, Bowring Park was opened by His Royal Highness the Duke of Connaught. Bowring

Brothers continued to make improvements and to pay for its upkeep until 1922, when it was deeded to the city under the control of an advisory board of seven members: his Worship Mayor Carnell (Chairman), Deputy-Mayor Spratt, Councillors Kelly and Vardy, Mr. Eric A. Bowring (representing the firm), Sir Leonard Outerbridge, Mr. D.R. Thistle, and Mr. J.J. Maloney as secretary.

Sir Edgar took a great interest in the park, making gifts and contributing to expenses and improvements. The late W.F. Canning, a Fellow of the Royal Horticultural Society, succeeded Mr. Cochius as curator of the park and did much to give it the distinctive qualities it has today: a natural park whose beauty is second to none on this side of the Atlantic.

COUNCIL CONSCIOUS OF ITS DUTIES

Over a period of years it has taken over $200,000 to develop this beautiful spot. Under the care of the St. John's Municipal Council and the watchful eye of the Advisory Board, the work of beautifying the park continues. This year's budget allocated $30,000 for upkeep. A retread asphalt road has been laid, eliminating dust. The latest addition is a driveway to the right as you pass over Waterford Bridge where motorists may park their cars in safety while they visit the park. Special attention is paid to children at all times, and the police keep vigilant watch. No hooliganism is tolerated and very rarely are acts of vandalism committed.

ATTRACTIONS AT THE PARK

Its virgin woodland retained as far as possible and its natural streams enhanced by rustic bridges, Bowring

Park boasts its beauty as its main attraction. With samples of many different types of trees and flower beds, students of nature find much to delight them.

The park, however, caters also to the sightseer, the sports lover, the picnic-minded, the hot and weary, the hungry and thirsty.

At the right of the driveway, settled among trees, is the home of the present park superintendent, Mr. Harry Hamlyn. It is interesting to note that both this house and the Bungalow were constructed and sent to this country in pieces which were assembled on the spot. Pre-fabricated houses are much talked of today, but at that time such a venture was unusual.

Swinging your car to the right (if you propose to drive through the park), you can catch a glimpse of the tree planted by the Duke of Connaught on the occasion of the opening of the park.

The delight of many of the sports lovers who visit the park is the excellent tennis court in the valley. There, too, will be found facilities for the enjoyment of the children. Swings, shutes and climbers attract crowds of youngsters. There too, by the side of the river, one may "boil up" for a cup of tea, dig into the picnic basket and sit in the shade of a tree to enjoy a snack.

Catering to those who love ice-cream and Coke, the Bungalow attracts huge crowds on its lawns. Homemade cookies and pastries can be purchased, and on slow days even afternoon tea.

The swimming pool is a great attraction for city-dwellers who have little opportunity for swimming. A paddling pool is available for the younger fry. The water is tested, the pool is cleaned regularly and is looked after by two caretakers. Newly constructed is an attractive bridge of beach stones just below the swimming pool.

The newest attraction will be the addition of swans to grace the placid lake. These are expected to arrive shortly.

MONUMENTS

Imposing and lifelike, the Fighting Newfoundlander, a monument presented by Sir Edgar Bowring as a tribute to the deeds of the Royal Newfoundland Regiment (1914-18), was unveiled in 1922 by His Excellency the late William Horwood. The figure, depicting a soldier holding a bomb with one hand while the other clutches a rifle, was posed by Corporal Thomas Pittman and is the work of the sculptor Basil Gotto.

Presented by Major W.H. Greene as a tribute to his comrades of the Regiment, the Caribou monument was unveiled in 1928 by His Worship the Mayor, Hon. Tasker Cook. It is a replica of a monument which stands in Beaumont Hamel Park, France. Natural and lifelike, it sits in its sylvan setting on the summit of a natural hillock.

Best loved is a statue of Peter Pan, which stands on the lawn bordering the lake at the entrance to the park. The sculptor, Sir George Frampton, made a visit to oversee the placement of the statue, a replica of one standing in Kensington Gardens, London. There are just three of these in the world. The statue depicts the Peter Pan of Sir James Barrie's classic, playing his pipes. Embellished with squirrels, mice, rabbits, fairies and other woodland folk, the pipes are drawing them all upward in fascination and delight. This statue was presented to the children of Newfoundland by Sir Edgar Bowring "In memory of a dear little girl who loved the park." On the inscription is engraved the name of Betty Munn, who was drowned in the *Florizel* disaster of 1918.

The latest monument to be presented is a statuette of John Cabot which can be found inside the Bungalow on the right-hand side of the fireplace. This was also presented by Sir Edgar Bowring.

CHURCHILL PARK AREA GRADUALLY BECOMING POPULATED (1947)

The Evening Telegram has gathered a cross-section of opinion from interviews with householders living in Churchill Park, in the St. John's Housing Corporation area.

The majority of finished houses are now occupied. The gardens in the lower village are landscaped, and trees have recently been planted so that this section is beginning to take on a very attractive appearance, a fulfillment of the prediction that this would be a "garden suburb" of St. John's. A few residents fear, however, that the landscaping at the rear of their houses will receive a serious setback if garbage trucks persist in tracking down through the neat tiers of topsoil.

COST OF HOUSES AND UPKEEP

A few street lights have been set up to the relief of residents who have been finding it very dark going at night. Although there are families who have lived in the area for nearly a year, there is still no postal delivery.

The majority of householders are well satisfied with their "bargains" despite the high cost of the houses. Actually, few people living there can afford the $10,000 to

$14,000 houses, and only the easy financing at moderate interest rates have induced them to take up the burden of monthly payments. The average house costs $11,500, plus the land, which runs to about another thousand dollars. The average man paid down a thousand dollars on his house, agreeing to pay $65 or $70 in monthly payments over a thirty-year period. Some, of course, have undertaken to pay off in twenty years and some have made an initial payment of well over a thousand dollars.

Rent includes approximately $3 in insurance based on the cost of the house, a fixed maintenance fund of $5 a month which may be drawn on for repairs, and city taxes amounting on average to just over $4 a month. Taxes are based on the assessed value of the property.

The average family finds the monthly payments none too easy to meet, with the exception of families who have had over the past few years to pay an exorbitant rent. In these cases, the families are saving not only on rent but on fuel.

HEATING SYSTEM EFFICIENT

The central heating system is efficient and cheap. Its greatest drawback is that so many gadgets have not yet turned up, and second-hand motors and thermometers have had to be installed until such time as the article can be obtained. Since most of the occupants expect the arrival of these gadgets, the inconvenience is now being borne by the householder rather than the Housing Corporation.

The bitterest months of winter found about five gallons of oil consumed per day. Many people burned less. This, in many instances, provided the only outlay for fuel with the exception of electricity. The popularity of the electric range is growing with the discovery that these houses can be kept quite warm and comfortable with the heating system, and the use of oil or coal in the kitchen for additional heating purposes is unnecessary.

DELAY IN MATERIALS

Ventilation presents a problem to the householder whose home is fitted with louvres. These are fitted with inside shutters which fold back to admit air. Unfortunately, the necessary hardware has not yet arrived. Consequently, the housewife has to remove one of the boards of the shutter whenever she wants her window open, and nail it up again when she wants it closed.

Occupants who have been living in Churchill Park, some of them since last July, have experienced considerable inconvenience through this, and are fearful that constant tampering with the shutters may result in damaging the windows. The Housing Corporation, it is understood, expects to have the hardware installed shortly.

PLANS ARE SATISFACTORY

From the viewpoint of the housewife, the layout makes for easier family living, although many residents do not care very much for the average layout, where kitchen, dinette and living room are not separate entities but run one into the other. However, the fear expressed by many that kitchen odors might permeate throughout the house has proved groundless, since the air-conditioning system rids the flat of cooking odors within ten minutes.

Some homes have an inferior grade of wallboard which has defied all efforts to paint properly. The hardwood floors are the bane of many a housewife's life, partly because new floors are difficult to "work up," and partly because householders contend that the wood is of inferior grade, is not seasoned, and was not treated properly after being laid.

Basements are extremely roomy. A few residents complain of water in the basement whenever it rains heavily, but such instances are not common. Many families plan to build up their basements so as to provide extra bedrooms, playrooms and laundries.

AREA STILL UNDER CONSTRUCTION

Practically every housewife interviewed complained of the excessive mud during bad weather and dust in dry weather, and expressed a yearning for the day when the streets will be properly constructed with the rubble and debris removed. At present the area is still under construction.

Only a few houses had storm doors at back and front during the winter. The average home, however, finds them a necessity. More homes would have been equipped with them this past winter but for the fact that it was some time before residents realized that the onus for placing these doors rested upon them. By that time, it was well into winter and doors were difficult to obtain. Most householders prefer a combination of storm and screen door.

HOUSEWIVES PLEASED

With remarkably few exceptions, the women living in the area would be reluctant to leave their homes despite the continued drain on the income. The chief drawing card was, in the first instance, the easy financial arrangements. Once the housewife has experienced the comfort and convenience of the home, she is very happy with her abode. Many complain, however, of the roughness of the skirting boards and the difficulty of cleaning dust from rough wood. Houses are very compact, making for speedier, easier house cleaning, though many regret the absence of a small hall at the front of the house. Although few want to leave, probably more than a few would not have moved there had houses been available elsewhere.

HAS RELIEVED SHORTAGE

The Housing Corporation project has undoubtedly relieved the housing shortage in some measure. Yet despite the new supply, there is still a shortage, even though several of these new houses are still awaiting occupants.

About half of the houses have a garage. Most residents use the Golden Arrow bus, which runs as far as Elizabeth Avenue. The service has not been all it might be, residents complain, partly because of the hour between runs, partly because buses seem to think it is their privilege to break down frequently. Nevertheless the service is appreciated. It takes a resident twenty minutes to walk to Water Street, allowing twenty-five for the return.

RESIDENTS ARE PLEASED

Apartments are cheaper than houses. The rent for these is $75-80 a month. With hot water and central heating provided, as well as an electric range, there is a saving of about $10-15 a month. However, apartments do not have the added attraction of a private garden, nor of course is the dweller acquiring an equity in a house. Individual homes have about one-sixth of an acre of land with a small lawn in front.

Whether or not the Housing scheme is a paying proposition, it has not been the purpose of this article to determine. However, it may be said that from the angle of the residents, the venture has proved satisfactory.

PART II: POST-CONFEDERATION WRITING

THE WHELPING ICE[30] (1952)

This story won second prize in the Short Story category of the 1952 Arts and Letters competition. While at first glance this seems to be just another sentimental romance, a closer look reveals a reversal of the traditional gender roles found in chivalric romances. The "patriarch" of the community and its pillar of strength is a woman; and it is a woman who rescues a lad in distress.

Dora also earned second prize in the Margaret Duley Fiction Contest, sponsored by the Newfoundland Writers Guild in 1974. While I cannot confirm this, it seems likely that the award was for a story entitled "One Good Turn."[31]

They stood together on the stage head, Big Martha and the small, shrivelled old man. Big Martha, they had always called her, as long as old Skipper Sam could remember.

Generations of Newfoundland fishermen, small of stature but wiry and hardy, had unaccountably bred this big-muscled, broad-shouldered woman, who stood six feet tall. She moved slowly and ponderously, but with unmistakable decisiveness. Every inch of her solid body expressed energy. Even her hair, which she wore short, shot out greying wisps that bristled with purposefulness and still shone with health.

[30] The term "whelping ice" refers to the ice-fields on which seals give birth.
[31] I am indebted for this insight to Tara Harris, an MA student at Memorial University whose thesis (1995) was entitled "A Study of Voice in the Writings of Dora Russell."

Skipper Sam could not remember a time when anyone in the Cove had gone against her. Down by the landwash, her big house was always open to friends and strangers alike, and she gave with a lavish hand. She had run her home efficiently, and with a firm hand, and the home had prospered. She had taken the business out of her husband's hands on his death, and it had prospered. The Cove knew her for a strong, harsh woman, but one to whom you turned in trouble, whose word was law, and whose laws were wise. She was independent and dependable, and the equal of any two men in the place.

Skipper Sam Hown lowered his ancient rear slowly to rest upon the edge of the upturned punt. Big Martha's slightly hardened eyes surveyed her property - the two strong wharves pointing their length into the now frozen waters, the fish-drying flakes perched atop the rocks and crags of the shoreline, the huge splitting table on the tip of the stagehead, the red-painted fish and salt stores.

"Sam," she said firmly, "I've never been wrong, and I'm not wrong now. Josh'll get over it. He'll have to. I've built up this business with my own two hands" - she extended two muscular hands in an unconsciously dramatic gesture - "and Josh will have to run it when I'm gone. I'll have no perfumed, book-readin' schoolteacher running my house and my business when I'm not here to do it myself."

The old man shifted his stern for'ard a good two inches, edging for a more comfortable position along the boat's bottom.

"Maybe you an't often wrong, Martha," he agreed amiably, "but I don't know as you be always right, neither. Don't know as all your proddin' an ambitionin' did poor old Jeremiah much good, God rest his soul. He warn't happy doin' big business for 'e."

"He didn't have to be," retorted Martha sharply. "I seen to all that. He'd nothing to fret his mind over."

Sam was silent, remembering Jeremiah. Remembering his gentling eyes that loved to look out to sea, his gentling fingers that itched to haul a codtrap and grasp a handbarrow. Sam guessed he knew more about his friend, dead these nineteen years, than his wife ever had. It had killed something in Jeremiah to give up the sea in order to tend the counter of the small trading store. Jeremiah had lived with and by the smell of sea air and fresh caught fish. Such a man could not take kindly to the strange smells of a general trading store.

True, the shop had grown, the small home on the hill had been abandoned in favour of the big, draughty house on the landwash, with two servant girls to keep it clean, and coal come clear over from Sydney to keep it warm. The business had grown, and with it, Martha's ambition to trade in fish.

"Ye've done a man-size job," admitted Sam, "but then, ye're a man-size woman."

He saw the muscles of Martha's arm grow taut as her fists tightened. "If I was to give you a clout, you wouldn't be the first to feel the weight of me hand, Sam Hown," she shouted at him. Martha liked to manage, and she glorified in her strength, but she took exception to anyone else alluding to it.

"Maybe Carrie Moncton an't got much muscle in her arm," remarked the old man slyly, "but she got sense in her head, and she'm stuffed wi' edication. We an't got enough edication hereabouts."

"I got along without much of it," returned Martha shortly. "Where would the people of this Cove be today if it weren't for me taking the fish off their hands? Carrie Moncton wouldn't know a jigger from a live caplin. She'm no good for Joshua. He needs a maid that an't afraid of her own shadder."

Skipper Sam shifted his tobacco chew from one wrinkled cheek to the other, and squirted a stream of brown juice over the stage head. He squinted against the glare of the high March sun on the frosted waters. He looked at the round red face of his best friend's wife, and thought of his best friend's son. Jeremiah would want Josh to marry the pretty young thing who had taught in the Cove school all winter.

"Ye be a wunnerful manager, Martha, tallyin' up all them accounts and doin' real business wi' the big people in St. John's. But, thar's more to livin' than turnin' the hay and splittin' the fish."

There was a silence between them, heavy and resentful, with something of sorrow in it too. The old man's stained grey whiskers, sharp and brittle with the years, moved tautly up and down with the motion of his jaws. His dark eyes, set on a mound of apple-red cheek, lifted to the tip of a snowy crag jutting high above the point of land. They followed the movements of the watcher atop who had been looking out to sea and who now turned to make his way slowly down the hill.

"Warn't no call for Josh to climb the Lookout," remarked Sam mildly. "I could've tole'n, thar's no whelpin' ice near yet. Won't see nary a sight o' swiles till the wind shifts to the east'ard, and well 'e knows it. Up thar, frettin' his heart out, what's what he's doin'."

"He've fret his heart out afore this." Martha turned her back on him. "But I've took note that he've always come out of it. He'll come out of this, too." She began to take massive strides along the fish stage.

"Heard tell teacher's leavin'," commented Sam, with a sly flick of the eye toward the broad buttocks.

Big Martha stopped in her tracks. "No. Never heard a sound."

"It be true. She'm not comin' back to the Cove in the fall. Heard tell she was leavin' Newf'nland altogether. Goin' across to Canada, what they calls the Mainland now, like it warn't Canada any more.

"Tain't no surprise," he continued, with another uncomfortable shifting of his rear end. "Seen it comin' a long spell ago. Shame. Carrie Moncton's the best teacher we'm had yet, for all her shy ways. She'm easylike in her manner, but them youngsters won't stand up to her like they done to t'others."

He filled in another uncomfortable pause. "Since the gov'ment got that darned bridge up," he fumed, "I an't got no livin' left at all. I be missin' the little maids and b'ys I used to ferry across the Tickle. Tell 'e somethin', Martha," and he leaned towards the big woman earnestly. "Thar's nary a winderpane been broke in school this year, not nobody's had no trouble wi' teacher. Seen Uncle Ben give his young un a lickin' for nippin' fresh billets off the woodpile. Last year, he couldn't get him to take his turn carryin' wood along t'school, and this year, he wants to bring the whole shebang wi' 'um. He even took part in the school concert. Could hear every word he said, and me at the back of the hall."

"Sam," said Martha with a hard stare. "All that may be true. I'm not sayin' a word against the girl, mind you. But them that teaches should stick to teachin'. Learnin' don't help gardens while the men is off to Labrador fishin'. First thing you know, Carrie Moncton would carry Josh off to St. John's or the Mainland. She'd never be content here. No sir. Josh is starting from the bottom, like me and Jeremiah did. He needs a wife what can stand to the splittin' table till two or three o'clock in the morning, like the rest of the women do, and then get up at six to start the house chores - not a fine lady wearing silk blouses to school, and readin' books right in the middle of the day."

She left him, and once more, Sam shifted his position on the overturned punt. He looked around for a target, selected a trawl-buoy, and thoughtfully scored a bull's eye.

Josh picked his way around the familiar area behind the schoolhouse. He was not a handsome man, but his keen sea-blue eyes and firm set of his mouth bespoke the strength of mind and body that sets the Newfoundlander apart from other men. Reaching a clearing, he made his way to his favourite boulder, wishing he could avoid the teasing eyes of the children but knowing that he couldn't. He settled himself on the rock within sight of the schoolhouse and made himself a cigarette.

Carrie was his first girl. He had not yet acquired ease in approaching her. In spite of her assurance that she loved him, he almost feared the very beauty of her. Accustomed all his life to rough work and rough ways, he found her loveliness and the dignity of her ways almost overpowering. It seemed too good to last. Anyone like

Carrie would surely never marry and live in a little outport, away from the comforts that made living easier. She was meant for better things, for a more gracious way of living, and he was conscious of a sense of guilt whenever he looked ahead to their life together.

No sooner had he regretfully disposed of his cigarette stub than the children began to stream from the school door in the greatest of spirits. Josh pretended not to notice the knowing glances and uncontrolled giggles that greeted him. Everybody knew. The walls of the schoolhouse and the neatly painted fence declared to all and sundry that such a dainty little person should care for an uncouth hulk of a man like him. Silently, the lovers linked hands, and turned homewards. The feel of her soft little hand in his roused Josh to a tenderness and protectiveness such as he had never known before. He savoured the loveliness of the feeling which had swept over him. Then, tearing himself away from the magic of the moment, he dropped her hand.

"It didn't work, Carrie," he said despondently. "Mother won't stand for it. I told her outright that I was going to marry you, no matter what. She said - she said - that if I did, I would no longer be son of hers."

"But what reason has she?" faltered Carrie. "I'd be a good wife to you. I know I would."

Josh stopped and took her tenderly in his arms. "I know you would, sweet," he murmured. " I know you would."

"What does she have against me?" demanded Carrie, pushing herself reluctantly from him. "It's not my fault that I'm educated, or that I was brought up in a city instead of an outport."

"She's just plain stubborn," answered Joshua. "Once she makes up her mind, there's no changing her. She has set her heart on my taking over the fish premises, and she has decided that I should marry someone who would help me as she helped my father."

Carrie shrugged her shoulders. "I," she remarked, "am not completely witless. I can learn the fish business. I can do whatever I must do."

"I know that, darling," he returned, capturing her small hands again and holding them carefully within his own. "But she's set in her ways. She's been cock of the walk so long that now, everything must go her way. There's only one thing to do. We must get married anyway. We can go away somewhere. She'll come around some day. She'll have to. After all, I'm all she has."

Carrie nodded, her eyes full of tears. "But don't you see, darling, that's just why we can't. We can't do this to her because, like you just said, you're all she has. I can't take you away from her altogether."

Josh's face hardened. "It's that or nothing, Carrie."

"Then Josh, it will have to be nothing. I couldn't start our married life together like that, knowing your mother resented me, despised me as a weakling, felt me to be unfit for her son's wife."

"But what about me, what about our love? Isn't that the most important thing of all?"

"No, Josh," she answered slowly, "it's not. Can't you see it as I do? I want to live happily with you. How can I, in the face of your mother's opposition? She would turn everybody against me, make life unbearable for me. I - - I couldn't face it."

"Not even for me?" he looked at her disbelievingly.

"Not even for you, Josh. Oh, believe me, it isn't that I don't love you. I do, more than I can say. But it's because I love you and want to be happy with you that I couldn't bear to make living intolerable for you. You think the world of your mother, dear. You'd be miserable if she cut you out of her life. You two have always been so close. And I can't be the one to bring you unhappiness. No, I can't marry you. Not unless your mother changes her mind about me."

"Is that your last word?" demanded Josh huskily.

She faced him squarely. "Yes, Josh. That's my last word."

He turned and left her abruptly. She looked after him, a fierce hard lump burning in her throat. Then she went on her way, alone.

In the house down by the landwash, Big Martha sent her two servants scurrying. Off came the mattress covers, the antimacassars and the furniture covers beneath the antimacassars. The homemade barrel rocking chairs were stripped of their bright chintz and tasseled cushions. Old socks and pieces of material, put carefully aside for hooking mats, were dumped and sorted. Down came crystallized calendars, their pockets stripped of buttons and pins and church envelopes. The hooked mats were taken up, the canvas removed from the floors. Cupboards were stripped and shelves laid bare. The big hanging lamp with its beaded fringe was carefully taken down from the parlour ceiling, the organ was stripped of its photographs and the sideboard bared of its ancient dishes. Pots of water filled the shining top of the big black victoria range.

This, however, was no ordinary spring cleaning day. This was Wash Day at Big Martha's. Like Christmas, it came but once a year. The word quickly got around that Martha had started this very morning to clear the rooms. The whelping ice can't be far off now, the women laughed. Martha always gets her spring wash done just before the seals come in.

Good humouredly, they dropped their own work, laid aside their plans for the day, and took out their buckets and scrub brushes. There would be plenty of work for all in that great rambling house. But there would be plenty of lively talk too, and afterwards the big celebration.

There might be a hard day's work ahead, but there would also be the reward of an honest day's labour. There would be fancy buns and pies and sweet figgy loaf. There would be blueberry wine and rice wine and corn whisky, and there would be Screech, brought in especially from St. John's for the men who liked a good drop of grog. There would be feasting and square dancing until daylight.

And so the women of the Cove gathered in twos and threes at Martha's house, though not without casting anxious eyes at the sky.

"Wind's comin' in nor'east. Looks like Big Martha's wrong for once. If there's any sign of swiles today, reckon the Big House will be left in a wunnerful mess."

Indeed, the last bucket of water had scarcely been drawn from the well when the watcher on the Lookout was seen to turn and half run, half slip down the slope, waving his arms. His shouts came but faintly to the ear but their meaning was unmistakable. "The ice is in. The whelping ice. Look, away to the east'ard. The seals. The seals."

Seals: a good winter's living. Seals: comfort, security. A new black dress for Grandma, and a set of uppers for Pap when the dentist came around that summer. A new organ for the church and the Parson's roof mended. Money for coarse salt and money for Screech. Money for fish nets and money for long rubber boots. Money to keep your name on the doctor's books and money for oranges and toys, come Christmas. The blessed black patches out yonder. The blessed seals.

But seals would wait for no man, and clearly, Martha's wash would have to wait. The Cove dove into a headlong rush. Men dropped the nets they were mending, the sails they were fashioning, and ran. Down to the landwash they ran, and out over the frozen sea. "Mind the clumpers, lads. No time to stumble over they." Out they ran, out to sea, out to the Eldorado of the whelping ice. And then, they were moving specks, and no woman's watching eye could tell which were seals and which were men.

Running as hard as any of them was Joshua, the bitterness in his young heart toughening his determination to get a good day's catch. As he ran, smoothly and effortlessly, his muscles rippled under the dark blue of his rough wool jersey.

A fine figure of a lad, thought Skipper Sam, as he mournfully watched the swift scurrying of men out to sea. Fit for any Newf'nlan' maid, he thought. Looked like he couldn't stand up to his mother, though. Well, a body couldn't rightly ridicule him for that. After all, he was a good man in a boat, even if he wouldn't take a drop of grog. Seven seasons fishing on the Labrador to his credit, too.

Joshua himself knew only a determination to forget his deep hurt, if only for a short time, in the taking of seals. A man's got no time to fret and worry when his sealing gaff is in his hand.

Reaching the patch of harps, he worked furiously, as did the men about him, for time was short. The male seals deserted their families in a twinkling, half writhing, half jumping over the ice in a clumsy gallop, flopping over its edges in frantic haste. The mother seals, who had just whelped, remained, as always, to die guarding their young. A blow or two from the sealing gaff was enough to make a kill, and the men had long ago become hardened to the pitiful, half human whimpering of the young whitecoats.

Soon the ice was red with the kill, and the day wore on.

Back in the Cove, the day's routine was disrupted. Who could wash and clean and scrub on a day like this? Martha herself abandoned her pile of blankets and joined the women gathered along the landwash.

Gradually the day settled into a restless routine of watching, of speculating, of making some pretence of work. The path to the tip of the Lookout had been worn smooth by generations of eager watchers. Nor was it neglected this day.

In the schoolroom, Carrie Moncton, fair of hair and firm of mouth, kept her restless class in order. Wisely, from time to time, she allowed a recess, when pencils were thrown hurriedly to desks as small feet scrambled to reach the choice positions at the window.

Skipper Sam, pacing the landwash, anxiously raised his eyes skyward. There wasn't a doubt of it, now. A southwest wind was freshening. A fissure jagged its length along the shore, it widened, and Skipper Sam started for the guns.

Slowly, the wind edged the ice out of the Cove, pushing it forward, out into the open sea.

A wild wave to those atop the Lookout in charge of the signal guns. A wild pointing to the strip of widening water, and then the guns sounded. Three straight quick blasts to warn the hunters that danger threatened, that they must slip their seals and run for their lives.

Women, at the sound of the signal gun, stopped in their tracks, then ran to the shore, calling out prayers at sight of the black water, at the slowly retreating ice, the monster ice, biding its time to trap their men. They moved about, helpless under an emergency that would allow them to do nothing to help. They wrung their hands. They muttered prayers. But they did not scream nor shout nor shed tears. If this dreadful thing had to happen, then it was the will of the good Lord.

Carrie Moncton came, to stand white-faced and quiet with the other women. The children had been let out of school and were peppering the shore with noisy and excited questions.

The swiftly running men drew nearer. The water widened. Slowly the ice drifted outward, and with deadly sureness. Farther along, long leads of water channelled out. Bits of ice broke off and drifted loosely about small ponds of water.

"Off wi' the boats," Big Martha suddenly galvanised into action. Down scrambled Skipper Sam, his old legs moving surely along the well-known rocks and crevices. Now all took up the refrain. Here was something to be done. No need yet of inaction, of wringing hands and worried faces. The boats had to be launched.

But the boats had, months before, been drawn up on shore. They were firmly imbedded in the hardened snows, loath to leave their winter's resting place. However, under the urgent pressure of many hands, they slowly yielded, and were pushed, pulled and jostled creakingly to the water's edge, where reddened hands frantically knocked oars to loosen the ice, and children stood knee deep in the icy water to give them a final heave. Long before the last boat dipped its nose into the water, the first of the string of punts, manned by Skipper Sam, was making its way towards the receding ice, at the edge of which stranded men waited, their piles of seals long since forgotten.

The south-westerly wind was beginning now to rise to gale force. It was not too soon, when finally the boats reached the ice and the men were taken on board.

Big Martha's face wore a relieved grin as she watched the returning boats. Forgetting her animosity in her relief, she turned to exchange a glance with Carrie. But Carrie was gone. Martha saw her scurrying off over the hills beyond, and wondered. Then she knew, and her face slackened with sudden age. Jim Dea was coming in, his two boys with him. Uncle John Wiggs was there, already waving his great long arms in greeting. Almost every man in the Cove had been out there that day, and they were all coming back.

All except Joshua.

The cry Martha gave was inaudible. There were so many lusty shouts of welcome, so much half hysterical gaiety, that even when her strong fingers gripped

Skipper Sam's arm, he saw her lips moving without hearing a sound from them. But there was no doubt as to the word she mouthed. He swung around.

"Where's Josh?" he shouted. "Ye've been and come back wi'out un."

"Back into the boats!" Martha found her voice at last, and was the first to jump into the nearest boat. Seizing the oars, she had pushed the punt off into the black waters again, before the tragic plight of the marooned man had been understood. Another boat quickly followed.

The gale was increasing steadily in force. Small children, finding difficulty in keeping their feet against the biting strength that tore about them, whimpered behind their mothers' skirts. But the wind was a blessing to Martha, and her boat sped smoothly forward.

"She better not put that punt too far out," someone worried. "Mind what happened to Dan's boys three springs ago. Wind took un clear out to sea. Never was seen since."

There was scant comfort, however, in the knowledge that the wind was helping to blow the two boats out to the rescue, since the same gale was also sweeping Joshua, alone on a pan of ice, out to sea. Beyond the south of the Cove, and at the end of a stretch of shore, a long point lent a final protective shelter. A bare mile off, there was a tiny island. Farther out, the Atlantic Ocean lashed and stormed and fretted in useless motion. The sweep of the wind was pushing the ice out and beyond this island, on into the ocean. Once past this point of land, there was no hope for any man. The boats with their straining, panting occupants had small hope of reaching Josh in time.

It was neither knowledge or seamanship nor sense of strategy that led the pretty young schoolteacher to leave the waiting crowd down by the landwash and scramble over the snowy hill separating the Cove from Western Point. She had known, long before the faces in the oncoming boats were recognizable, that Joshua was not there. The same instinct that had warned her of his danger had also shown her the only hope there was of saving him.

She understood the danger perfectly. If the wind and the tide forced the ice through the tickle that lay between Western Point and the island, there was hope. But if it were forced along the other side of the island, she would have to watch helplessly while Joshua drifted out of her sight and out of her life forever. No boat, she knew well, could follow him into the tearing gale that raged outside the sheltered cove. The great winds would sweep him out to a lonely death.

Carrie continued her mad scramble over slippery rocks and snow-filled hollows. The length of rope she had instinctively grabbed from someone as she left was hampering her progress. She fell often, tangling herself in the rope, losing precious minutes. Finally, when it seemed that one more tumble must surely break her will to carry on, she came within sight of the sea. Before her lay the long length of the Point, with the tiny island just off its tip. And there, drifting on his solitary pan of ice, was the lone figure of Joshua.

Now that the end was in sight, for better or for worse, Carrie drew on some hidden reserve of strength. She slithered over the ice coated rocks, once familiar and dear on those sunny Sunday afternoons when she and Joshua had wandered together there, but strange and threatening now.

There was no time to pick and choose her way. She kept going blindly, praying that soon she would reach the uttermost tip of the Point. She dared not risk raising her eyes to the lonely figure, dared not risk wasting the breath it would have to take to cry out an encouraging word to him. The last few yards had seemed such an interminable distance that she looked disbelievingly at the chopping seas that washed near her as she slid down to the beach.

Joshua had seen her now, was waving to her. The pan of ice neared the tip of the island, edging to the northerly side. Joshua was using his gaff frantically, uselessly trying to push the ice so that it would pass southward, and into the comparative safety of the tickle. Carrie shut her eyes. A great shudder swelled from the pit of her stomach to her throat, but the scream that was building itself never broke from her. Instead, she fumbled for the rope. The ice was edging slowly towards the island.

There was no difficulty in locating a suitable boulder. The beach was strewn with them, and they jutted out from the winter's snowfalls like white pillars of strength. As quickly as her numbed fingers would allow, she tied one end of the rope firmly around a boulder and fumbled for the other end. Her eyes, alive with terror, searched for her lover's position.

He was nearing her. She could see the drip of water on his clothes, the grin on his daredevil face, and she took fresh courage.

She had never thrown a rope before in her life, but she threw one now with unerring aim towards the pan of ice. Joshua picked it up with a swift movement. She watched the rope tighten as he wound it quickly in, watched his body stiffen as he pulled.

Her throat welled with terror again. She went back to the boulder to watch the rope's straining tautness. Now he was slowly, oh so slowly, pulling himself in, his legs planted firmly apart on the tiny pan of ice. At each powerful tug, the rope strained and quivered. But it held, until with a leap, Joshua bridged the remaining gap of water and was beside her, panting, stumbling, but safe and sound in her arms.

"You'll never leave me now," he gasped, as he held the tiny, shuddering figure firmly against his ice-laden shoulders.

"Nobody got a'ar seal," was Big Martha's comment, when the women gathered the next morning to commence her spring wash. "But I reckon Josh got hisself a good maid for a wife. Time this Cove had some edicated people living in it." And she glared defiantly at their smiling faces.

Dora's paternal grandparents,
Josiah and Mary Ann (Hines) Oake, Change Islands.

Dora's parents: Jesse and Laura (Brinson) Oake.

Dora in front of the Oake family home, St. John's, c. 1930.

Dora and her new husband Ted Russell, St. John's, 1934.

Annie Saunders, who provided domestic help for Dora during the years in Springdale. Children: Betty (in arms) and Rhona (standing).

House in Harbour Breton where Ted and Dora lived in 1939-40.

Dora in Woody Point, Bonne Bay with two of her children
(Betty standing, and June in arms.)

Dora holding June, Topsail, 1943.

Ted and Dora dressed for "on the town" in 1950.

Dora with two of her daughters, Peggy and June, St. John's.

Dora preparing to leave for work, St. John's, c. 1955.

A relaxing moment for a busy working mother.

Dora holding Peter Rabbit, an unusual family pet, 1961.

In Joe Batt's Arm for the wedding of her daughter Betty, 1961.

Arriving by skidoo for the wedding of her daughter June, 1963.

The Russell family home in St. John's (Stoneyhouse St.)

The Russell family at Christmas:
l-r Rhona, Betty, Peggy (in front of Betty), Ted, June, Dora.

The centre of the Russell Christmas – the tree.

Dora with her only son Kelly.

Ted and Dora share an affectionate embrace.

Dora in her late-60s at her St. John's home.

TIDAL WAVE (1954)

On November 18, 1929, an earthquake measuring 7.2 on the Richter scale occurred on the southern Grand Banks. It was followed by a tsunami comprising three major waves that struck close to forty communities on the Burin Peninsula, Hundreds of homes and businesses were lost along with, tragically, twenty-eight lives. The disaster was compounded by the fact that communication with the outside world was lost.

(FADE IN MUSIC – FADE OUT)

Twenty-five years ago, a tidal wave struck the south coast of Newfoundland, leaving death and destruction in its wake …

(FADE IN MUSIC)

NARRATOR 1 (as music fades out)

The houses always looked safe enough, clinging to the bare rocks, their wooden shores holding them aloft with steady strength. They had squatted tenaciously on those rocks these many years, and wind and rain had not harmed them. Who was to dream that such a thing as a tidal wave could ever desecrate the coast of Newfoundland? But it came. From the very sea bottom it came, rearing high, like a monster with salt dropping lips, flinging itself on our flakes of fish, tossing away our boats, our cod traps, our fish stores. It came, heaving itself inshore, throwing away toy houses like so much trash, and sucking toy people into its yawning maw. Then, retreating, sly monster creeping, slithering guiltily back into its haunts. (PAUSE) And all we had went with it.

(FADE IN MUSIC AND FADE OUT)

NARRATOR 1

1929 - a year of disaster the world over. 1929 - when the stock markets crashed and millionaires became paupers overnight, when people in millions joined the bread lines and crowded the soup kitchens. Newfoundland too, bore its share of the strain of depression. There was a drop in fish prices, bringing ruin to thousands of islanders.

But, to the people of the Burin Peninsula, memories of all such tragedies fade, in the face of the one memory that will always remain …

(FADE OUT VOICE)

NARRATOR 2

It was a fine cool afternoon in the fall of 1929, November 18, a Monday. We on the Burin Peninsula will never forget the dreadful horrors of that night, when the great tidal wave forced us to the hills for refuge.

We felt the tremor of the earthquake about a quarter past five, and we talked of nothing else around the supper table. After a while, we put it out of our minds and turned back to the ordinary business of living.

It was about half past seven when the tidal wave struck.

There were men down on the wharves and around the fish stores. There were women tidying up their homes and settling their children away to homework or bed. There were old folk nodding in their rocking chairs by cosy kitchen fires. There were women at the Parish Hall, arranging for a sale of work.

NARRATOR 1

The wave swept in from the Atlantic, striking swiftly and suddenly, with a deep indescribable roar.

(FADE IN CRESCENDO MUSIC WITH LAST WORDS. MUSIC REACHES PEAK AND CRASHED TO STOP. CONTINUES SOFT AND PIERCING SWEET IN BACKGROUND AS VOICE CONTINUES)

Almost instantaneously, the harbours and coves were sucked dry, and then the wave roared inland with a shuddering crash, later described as a noise like that of a squadron of airplanes in flight overhead.

The great fifteen foot wall of water beat on frail dwellings, dashed stores, wharves and fishflakes to splinters, tossed boats and vessels into the air. Houses were swept out to sea. (PAUSE, CONTINUING QUIETLY) And there were people in them.

NARRATOR 2

Like the Kellys!

FIRST VOICE (woman's)

'Tis gone. Kelly's house is gone. Look. See it there, on top of the wave, going out to sea. Oh, my God. Vince's wife and kids are in that house.

SECOND VOICE

No, they're out. Someone jumped out. It's the oldest one. She's got another one with her. Hey, fellows, down to the shore, quick.

FIRST VOICE

She's safe. She's safe enough. They're both safe. But oh, her poor Mom. She's still out there with the other child. (VOICE RISES) Oh, help them, somebody. Do something.

SECOND VOICE

Take it easy, take it easy. She may be found yet. The Kellys aren't the only ones to suffer. Ah, there's many a family will bear the marks of this night for years to come.

NARRATOR 1

Never a truer word was spoken. It was indeed years before the Peninsula recovered from the shock of that black Monday. A heavy gale which sprang up from the southeast the following day completed the work of destruction. And, to pile suffering upon suffering, the fisheries failed completely all along the stricken coast for the next five years.

NARRATOR 2

Mrs. Kelly and her child were never seen again. The house was sucked out through the Gut. Later that night, a crew put out to salvage what they could. They found the lamp still burning in the bedroom and the clothes pushed back on the bed as if the mother had snatched up her child. The only sign of life was the cat. Having pushed the other children to safety, Mrs. Kelly had apparently rushed back to snatch her baby from its bed and had probably jumped from the house, too late, as it was being carried out to sea.

SECOND VOICE

I was on a schooner that night. A bunch of us were on the *Daisy*. We were sitting around having a game of cards, when one of the hands came dashing in, calling out, "The town is sinking." We dropped our cards and got out on deck, quick. Sure enough, the town was sinking, as far as we could see. We were on top of the waves, way up above the Government wharf, and when the water rushed in to land, we all got off, right fast.

NARRATOR 2

There were many escapes that night. Like that of Fred Bartlett of Burin. (FADE OUT VOICE)

VOICE (Bartlett)

I was driving to Path's End at the time, and was near Penny's Bridge when I saw this huge wave coming towards me. I was in a fix. It didn't seem to matter much whether I went forwards or backwards. I suppose the natural instinct was to go ahead. Anyway, that's what I did. I gave her all the gas she would take, and she fairly flew over the bridge. I was barely across it when the wave struck. When I finally caught my breath enough to look back, there was the bridge, floating away behind me. It was a pretty bad moment, I can tell you, and it's just about impossible to describe the relief I felt when I realized the narrow escape I'd had. I never want to go through anything like that again.

NARRATOR 1

In the narrow channel at Penny Pond Bridge, the water rose to a great height and gouged a channel three or four feet deep out of the solid rock, tearing loose huge blocks of stone from the cliff.

VOICE (Coady)

I guess I had a pretty close shave, too, me and my family. We were lucky to get out of it alive.

I'm Luke Coady, from Corbin. I was just sitting around at the kitchen table when the whole house just lifted. It was lifted clear from its foundations and washed out into the harbour. I made for the back door, but the darned thing stuck and wouldn't open. That was a bad moment for all of us, to be stuck inside on account of that door. I was still tugging and twisting and straining at that blasted door when the house came back to shore. But she still wouldn't give, and out to sea we went again. We thought for sure we were gone this time, but we washed inshore again, and by that time I had the door smashed open. I grabbed up the two youngsters, one under each arm, and then I bawled to my wife to climb on top of my back. I jumped clear of the house, and we were some glad when we felt the solid ground under our feet. We certainly got God to thank that we were all saved that night.

NARRATOR 2

Then there was Walter Pike of St. Lawrence. He was holding on to his motor dory when the wave swept him out to sea. Another huge wave swept him back in and landed him at the very door of his house.

At Stepaside, a house with ten people in it was carried away, to the horror of those on shore. The cries went up: "Jump when the tide comes back." They did jump, and when the next wave pulled the house seawards again it drifted away with all its evidences of homely occupation. But the ten human souls that had gathered there that night had been saved.

Not so fortunate was a man of Port au Bras who was a short distance away from his house when the wave struck. Seeing the danger that threatened his home, he rushed back to save his wife and family. He might perhaps have succeeded, had not his path been blocked by another house which was floating by, and before his eyes, his home, with his imprisoned family, was whirled away into the darkness. Frantically, he looked about for a boat, but everything along the waterfront had been swept clean, nor could a boat live in that heaving sea.

The unfortunate man ran a mile to Bull's Cove, hoping by some miracle that the house would ground as it rounded the point, but it had, along with its unfortunate occupants, long since disappeared.

NARRATOR 1

Many such tragic incidents could be told of that disastrous night. A most graphic account was given by the Honourable George A. Bartlett, when he later arrived at St. John's, as part of a three-man delegation, to lay the situation before the Government, and seek aid for the stricken people ...

(FADE OUT VOICE)

VOICE (Bartlett)

Peering through the darkness, watching the receding waters, and hearing cries of distress from every quarter, I was appalled. The scene could not be described. Across the harbour at Kelly's Cove, stores were floating around everywhere in the backwash of the tide. People panic-stricken could be seen running here and there. (FADE OUT VOICE)

NARRATOR 1

In the midst of tragic incidents and narrow escapes, heroism played its part. Mr. Ray Hunter of Burin climbed on a floating building to rescue a woman with her family. A man named Antle, at Mortier, saved an elderly lady, but in smashing the windows in order to reach her, he severed a blood vessel, and almost bled to death before reaching Burin, seven miles distant, the nearest place where he could get medical attention.

NARRATOR 2

The people of the coast will always remember with affection and respect the efforts of Nurse Cherry of Nonia Centre, who was stationed at Lamaline. Nurse Cherry's devotion to duty during the horrible days that followed was an epic of tirelessness and selflessness and bears witness to the gallantry that has so often been evident among the members of her profession.

Another story of extreme devotion to duty is that of Miss Fewer, telegraph operator at St. Lawrence. Regardless of danger, she remained at her post and tapped on her keyboard a warning to the people of Burin. Minutes later, the tiny telegraph office tore loose and caught on a shoal in the middle of the harbour.

An eye witness account of the scene at St. Lawrence was later given by Mr. A.A. Giovannini, a resident of the place. (FADE OUT)

(FADE IN VOICE OF GIOVANNINI)

VOICE

The water would rise to a height of thirty to forty feet, and with the roar of the water and the cracking of timber, the spectacle was terrifying. On one or two occasions, with the receding tide the bottom of the harbour was clearly seen about half a mile from the mainland.

NARRATOR 1

Not all the incidents were as tragic as those described.

A store at St. Lawrence was swept away with its contents, but, to the great surprise of those around, it was washed back again and grounded near its original site.

At Port au Bras, the house of Mr. J.J. Abbott was washed out. In it were a crowd of men playing the good old Newfoundland game of Auction Forty-Fives. A second wave sent it floating back, practically on its original site, and the occupants scrambled out thankfully. When Mr. Abbott recovered from the impact of the shock, he found that he still had his cards in his hands. Nothing better illustrates the saving humour of the Newfoundland people than this remark: "My God," he said. "My house and all gone, and we were twenty-five in the hole!"

NARRATOR 2

In less than half an hour, the sea had done its worst. In darkness, with chaos everywhere, the men of the S.S. *Daisy* climbed on floating houses, searched among the debris, and rescued women and children. That night, and the following day, in a raging southeast gale and heavy seas, the ship and her gallant crew were doing the impossible, braving the angry elements to salvage boats and schooners.

NARRATOR 1

For three days, the plight of the people along the coast remained unknown. For three days, they took shelter where they could find it, treated their injuries as best they could, and ate what few supplies had not been sucked away by the sea. Heavy gales followed in the wake of the tidal disaster and wires were down all over the stricken Peninsula. It was the twenty-first of November when the S.S. *Portia* arrived at Burin, and through her wireless, the rest of Newfoundland learned with horror of the loss of twenty-eight lives and a terrific property damage amounting to a million and a quarter dollars.

Messages now began to pour in from the suffering settlements.

VOICE 1

Port au Bras. Seven people swept out of harbour. Eleven homes lost, fourteen small schooners, all dories and skiffs, and all waterside premises gone. Also five hundred quintals of fish lost and all the winter's provisions, fuel, traps and gear of every description. Great distress here. There is not five barrels of flour left in the place, and no coal. Huge boulders driven inland and large section of the beach carried away, rendering the harbour almost useless for shipping. Once a prosperous place, Port au Bras now in ruins.

VOICE 2

St. Lawrence. Great damage done but no lives lost. Thirty-one buildings swept away, all flakes and stores both sides of harbour completely destroyed, nearly all boats at Government wharf gone.

VOICE 1

Point au Gaul. Eight lives lost. All fishing property, stages and stores gone. Nearly a hundred buildings destroyed, a hundred tons of coal and all provisions. Three motor boats left of the thirty-five operating. Destitute here. Survivors suffering fearful ordeal.

VOICE 2

Taylor's Bay. Conditions indescribable. Wave between eighty and a hundred feet high here. Piers lifted bodily and thrown far inland in heaps of ruins. Houses shifted in every direction. Congestion dreadful. Five lives lost and fifteen families homeless. No vestige of waterside property left.

VOICE 1

Lord's Cove. Houses washed hundreds of yards inland and many swept to sea. Four lives lost.

VOICE 2

Lamaline. Thirteen people lost their lives. All stages and stores along the waterfront swept away.

VOICE 1

Lawn. All fishing property gone, with most of the boats and dories, provision and coal. No lives lost.

VOICE 2

Ship Cove. One house swept to sea with occupants, but was swept back again long enough to permit rescue.

VOICE 1

Stepaside. All waterside premises laid in ruins.

VOICE 2

Kelly's Cove. Two lives lost.

VOICE 1

Rock Harbour. Everything swept away. Tidal wave rose to considerable height, sweeping the narrows with great violence and carrying schooners and everything before it.

NARRATOR 2

An appeal for immediate relief was made by Magistrate Hollett[32], and the government of the day responded with prompt action.

Longshoremen threw themselves vigorously into the work of loading the S.S. *Meigle.* Supplies of food, bedding, clothing, glass and building materials were loaded aboard ship in record time. The steamer moved away from the pier with doctors and nurses on board, as well as members of the government.

[32] Malcolm Hollett (1891-1985) was a magistrate and politician. Elected to the National Convention in 1946, he was a strong supporter of responsible government. After Confederation, he served for a time as leader of the Progressive Conservative Party in the House of Assembly.

In a communication to the Colonial Secretary, the Honourable Dr. H.M. Mosdell, who was on the relief ship, described the conditions as he saw them along the coast.... (FADE OUT VOICE)

VOICE (Mosdell)

At Lord's Cove and Lamaline, the relief expedition found dozens of houses, stores and stages thrown bodily into ponds at the head of the harbours, huddled together in one heap of destruction. Some lay upright but half submerged, others lay on their sides and still others were entirely overturned. At Lord's Cove, a small house was seen right in the middle of a pond, hundreds of yards from its original site. In this tiny house, a mother and three children were caught downstairs by the rising wave, and drowned. Upstairs, a small baby lay in bed, and was taken out, entirely unharmed. The house of death now stands half submerged in water, isolated and desolated, its windows broken and its frayed white blinds fluttering in the breeze like a flag of distress.

NARRATOR 1

At no time in living memory has there arisen an emergency when the need of a combined community effort has been so urgent. At no time in living memory has such a combined effort been made more earnestly, more sympathetically, more selflessly than following the South Coast disaster. With the price of fish dropping from nine dollars a quintal to half that price, with the heavy hand of depression gripping the shoulder of every man, Newfoundlanders everywhere tightened their belts and dug down into what was left in their pockets. As in the great sealing disaster of 1914, almost as soon as the news was heard, donations began to pour in, from Newfoundlanders at home and abroad, from the Canadian and the American Red Cross, from people in England, Canada and the United States, from parish funds, from Water Street firms, from lodges, from ladies' aids, from Boy Scouts and Girl Guides, from thousands of individuals and hundreds of organizations. The Newfoundland Board of Trade was prompt in organizing public meetings and enlisting help, and the sum of $250,000 was soon raised.

Today, twenty-five years later, the unforgettable misery and horror of the Burin disaster is still fresh in the memories of those who went through those trying times. Long since have the lost homes been rebuilt, the wharves and fishing gear replaced. Long since have the people resumed their normal way of life. But lost ones are still mourned, and November storms never fail to recall the tragic incidents of that time and rouse the dreadful fear of re-occurrence in every breast.

(FADE IN MUSIC - FADE OUT)

IN DEFENSE OF REPORTERS (1954)

The relationship between Smallwood and the local press was uneasy, to say the least. The Premier's early targets were Ted Russell (who resigned from the Cabinet in March 1951) and Harold Horwood, a one-time supporter of Smallwood who, as political reporter and editor for The Evening Telegram, *became the Premier's most outspoken critic. Under the cover of House of Assembly privilege, Smallwood heaped one nasty epithet after another on his opponents in the Press: a contemptible cur, a snake, a crocodile, a loathsome scavenger, a card-cheat, an embezzler, a communist, a degenerate. By 1954, the Newfoundland Press Club had had enough of its honorary president. Spurred on by the Premier's actions to control how and when certain pieces of information would be released to the media, the Club expelled Smallwood. This attracted the attention of the* Northern Miner, *a Toronto-based industry newspaper which had itself been attacked by Smallwood and labelled "the most venial rag in all Canada." Writing about the Premier's expulsion, the editor quoted extensively from Dora's "In Defense of Reporters."*

I wish to make use of your column to say a few words that have needed airing for a long time. I am a political reporter. I wish to speak in defense of reporters.

The work of reporting sessions is exacting at the best of times. Contrary to the Premier's notion that precise reports should be given word for word, modern reporting demands that the gist of events be given and that newsworthy items be given preference. One cannot waste space by mentioning the name of every man who chooses to open his mouth. Of course it's been a long time since the days when the Premier himself reported, and one is led to believe that he must have been a very immature reporter, so slight is his grasp of modern requirements.

There is not, there has never been a reporter of the House sessions who was not anxious to do a fair and conscientious job. It is a reporter's instinct to merge himself into the very identity of the speaker he reports.

We make plenty of mistakes, mostly because the acoustics in the House are very poor, and because many of the members do not speak loudly or clearly enough or fail to present their material in an orderly fashion. The Premier, who is quick to draw the attention of the House to any talking on the opposition side while a member is speaking, makes no effort himself to display a similar courtesy. On more than one occasion, he has seated himself directly in front of the press box, there to carry on an audible conversation with some official.

Recently, Harold Horwood was the victim of an unwarranted blast of venomed spite and hatred such as has never before been heard in the House. Of course, it is a fact well known to observers that any hint of criticism drives the Premier to a frenzy that is horribly fascinating to watch. It doesn't seem human - or decent.

During this session, as well as in others, the Press has endured the vilification which the Premier has heaped upon it from beneath the skirts of privilege. Cowering securely behind this comforting barricade, he may say anything about anybody - and frequently does - with a cocky confidence that nothing he says will ever be used against him.

This reporter, and others who have aroused the antagonism of the Premier, must sit and take it. I myself have been verbally lashed by the Premier while doing nothing more subversive than my duty to my listeners.

It would be unreasonable to protest against any member's right to object to errors in reporting, for the sake of the record. It is a different thing entirely, however, when abusive, slanderous and damaging language is used under the protection of privilege. I deem this a most cowardly form of attack. Visitors from the mainland have, in my hearing, expressed their amazement at such conduct on the part of the Premier, stating that they have heard nothing remotely approaching it in any other provincial assembly. The Premier is doing nothing to correct any impression that Newfoundlanders are a mob of insular hillbillies.

In the House of Commons in Ottawa, Hansard may be consulted half an hour after the close of the sitting so that possible inaccuracies may be checked. In Newfoundland, a Hansard has not been published for four years, and there is reason to believe that this government does not intend to publish another. One can well understand its shame at not wishing the public to read a report of everything that has been said in the House.

Things have come to such a pass that a reporter hardly dares to quote the Premier at all, because what he says one day he emphatically denies the next.

My impression in relation to fees and salaries at the birch plant was that Mr. Hollett had been proved wrong.

I said so in my radio report. Harold Horwood was correct in saying that the Premier was wrong. My report was at fault in that respect.

We then had the curious situation in the House where the Premier dubbed Horwood's reporting a "deliberate lie," whereas the Opposition Leader [Hollett], who had certainly been "misrepresented" by me, was too well bred to make such a statement. We will never see the day when he will stand up in the House and call me, or any other reporter, a "loathsome literary rat." Ugh! The words make one shudder. Their use at all by a premier fills one with deep shame.

My personal opinion is that the parental hand should have been soundly applied to the Premier's anatomy when he was in his formative years - assuming he has ever outgrown them. In that event, he may by this time have been able to control as nasty and childish a temper as any man has been cursed with. He might even have learned how to exercise the control and dignity expected of a man in his position.

As the Premier has so often remarked, one can learn a great deal from pigs.[33] However, as teachers, pigs appear to have their limitations. They can impart only what they have.

And they do not have good manners.

FACTS ABOUT OUR SUPERSTITIONS (1956)

Superstitions are a curious and fascinating study. While they may appear on the surface to be just plain silly, a little examination reveals the fact that there are often sound reasons behind the seemingly unreasonable

[33] From 1943 to 1945, Smallwood had operated a pig farm in Gander.

beliefs held in times past and clung to in a surprising measure in Newfoundland today.

It is perfectly natural that superstitions should have swayed our reasoning powers. After all, where there is lack of knowledge, one can only conjecture; and people are just as frightened today of the unknown as ever they were. And they will continue to find some supernatural explanation for the things they cannot understand.

Maybe the war years made us less sensitive, but even today, many people will never pass under a ladder. Just in case. It's always better to be safe than sorry.

Usually, there is something behind a superstition. There is a perfectly reasonable explanation for this dread of passing under a ladder. Many years ago, malefactors were speedily removed from their sphere of activities by hanging them from a tree. But times changed. Towns grew up. Trees grew scarce. Eventually, ladders were slung against walls, and rope slung over a rung.

Many innocent men were lynched in those rough days, and one may safely assume that many attempts were made at rescue. The result was that any attempt by a passing stranger to go under a ladder was immediately regarded with suspicion as a possible rescue plan. Therefore, law-abiding citizens made it a rule to keep as far as possible from a ladder propped up against a wall. A perfectly sensible thing to do, in any case. The surprising factor is the way a custom holds on, long after the need for it has ceased. Truly, we are creatures of habit!

Other superstitions are not so easily explained. For instance, it is unlucky to bring certain flowers into the house, particularly lilacs. One might interpret this as an act of robbing nature of her glories, a selfish act that hides the beauty of the outdoors from the eyes of passers-by. But why lilacs?

Then again, you must never bring a single daffodil into the house. Always bring a bunch. Would this be because the daffodil bulb spreads freely, and if we are mean where nature is bountiful, we might cause offense to the powers that be?

There is an old superstition very much alive today that a heavy crop of red berries means a white and severe winter. This superstition is by no means common to Newfoundland, since in early times the holly, elder and other red berry trees were held sacred because of the plentiful harvest they gave, a harvest that provided food for the birds in winter.

This superstition *seems* to work out very well, but when you examine it, you realize that berries, like seeds, *must* be the result of *past* weather. However, it is a fact that nature seems to even things up in the matter of weather, and we usually find a fine, warm summer is followed by a sharp winter. So actually, a heavy crop of berries is due to the degree of warmth and rainfall of the summer and it so happens that nature, in its evening-up process, usually sends a sharp winter after the type of summer that produces a good berry crop.

Sailors are always a particularly superstitious lot. It is no cause for wonder then, that Newfoundlanders, in their close association with the sea, should have become a prey to the hundreds of odd beliefs that still prevail. Whistling on the water will bring wind, so you have to be careful not to overdo the musical effort or you may find yourself with more wind than you can comfortably handle. A whistling woman means bad luck. Would this be due to a resentment of feminine interference in masculine spheres? My mother always told me no lady ever whistled. That was strictly for the men. Be that as it may, seamen seem to prefer women in their proper places, and shipboard is not one of them. That brings bad luck too.

The Newfoundland fisherman has a firm belief in doing things *with* the sun. He turns his boat with the sun when leaving the wharf, never coils his rope against the sun. He deals cards with the sun. The reasons? Presumably because when the wind veers against the sun, it brings bad weather. And it doesn't take much imagination to link bad weather with bad luck!

A people living in isolation and without the benefits of medical attention will naturally cling to all sorts of odd beliefs in cures for their ills. Toothache, for instance, can be cured by applying pebbles from a newly made grave. A potato in the pocket will ward off rheumatism. A cake of hard tack carried in the pocket will protect one from the "fairies."

Warts may be got rid of by wrapping pebbles in a cotton rag, then throwing it away. With luck, someone else will pick up the bundle - someone, that is, who isn't wise to this particular piece of magic - and the warts will be transferred to the unlucky picker-upper. Or, a more kindly and neighbourly method is to transfer the warts to a cat. You do this by rubbing the wart with bacon rind and then feeding the rind to the unsuspecting puss. So, if you ever come across a cat with warts, you'll know what happened to the poor animal.

The first snowfall in May will cure sore eyes, as everybody knows, and lumbago may be cured by the simple expedient of lying on one's face and letting a woman named Mary step on one's back.

There are ways to be lucky at cards, too. Or at least, to avoid being unlucky. Just observe these few simple rules. Don't play cards with your hat off, as this is an act of homage to the Jack of Spades who, of course, is the Old One himself. Don't sit under a beam while playing, walk around the table to change your luck, and never lend money during a game.

Green is an unlucky colour, because it belongs to the "little people." The fire in St. John's in 1892 and the bank crash that followed two years later were said to have been due to the issue of green stamps for those years. If you are foolish enough to wear green, you may be carried off by the fairies at any time.

And don't scoff at the little folk! Many old people still say that they have seen fairies dancing on the grass on a moonlight night, and everyone knows that a child who has lost its way has been led astray by them. Of course, you may wear green and defy the fairy power, for if you carry a cake of hard bread in your pocket, you will be perfectly safe. This method is absolutely foolproof. Try it yourself and see!

There are a great many superstitions still prevalent regarding clothes. For instance, if you get up in the morning and put something on inside out, it's bad luck to change. On the other hand, if you have had a bad morning and feel it's time your luck changed, just go home and put on your underwear wrong way out. That will do the trick for you. Mind you, it won't necessarily bring you *good* luck, but it's supposed to put a stop to the bad luck.

If your toes go into the heel of your stocking first, you may expect a letter. If your stocking falls down, it means that someone you love is thinking of you. One would prefer to have this assurance in some less embarrassing manner, but there you are! There's no accounting for some superstitions. So it won't surprise you to learn that it is also unlucky to cross-button any article of clothing. Each fastener or button must go into its proper place, or else you are in for it!

We are all of us familiar with the superstition that you must always pick a pin up if you see one lying around, particularly on the ground. It's good luck. Personally, I think it's a piece of good luck to pick up anything that is of any use. It's all you'll ever get for nothing in a world that even pays for its air. This superstition is really a rather delightful bit of Eastern philosophy, meaning that it is better to bend the back for something useful than for nothing.

We've most of us tied knots in our handkerchiefs now and then, especially at berry-picking time. This act was originally intended as a charm against evil. The idea was that the knot would so intrigue the spirit that his attention would be fixed upon it, while you simply went your way unmolested. Nowadays of course, if one has a hankie and not a tissue, the knot is used to jog one's memory and can prove intriguing enough to the knotter who has forgotten why he ever tied it in the first place.

Perhaps you had forgotten that it is considered bad luck to look at the setting sun, or even talk about it. The idea behind this was that when the sun set, it was going into conference with the powers of darkness. It is also bad luck to turn a hatch cover upside down on deck or tear a flag, or mend or sew sails on the quarter deck of a vessel. Nor must you ever sail from port on a Friday or Sunday, nor reach port on a Saturday night. The reason for the latter may be a practical one, involving the poor sailor's purse. As to the former, Friday is naturally an unlucky day, and the history of Friday with its welter of bad luck would fill many, many pages.

Then it is considered risky to sail with a man who has neglected to pay his washerwoman before going to sea. As very few Newfoundland fishermen ever have any need to pay a washerwoman anyway, the moral of this superstition must be simply to pay your debts before venturing out on what may be your last journey.

It is bad luck too, to be the first to cross a new bridge, or be baptized in a new font, or to be buried in a new cemetery. So, whatever you do, be sure to guard yourself against this. Goodness knows what sort of misfortune might befall you, once you are beneath the sod!

CHRISTMAS AT OUR HOUSE (1962)

Almost every family, it seems to me, creates its own special Christmas customs and ceremonies over the course of its few years together as a unit. Traditions are always in the making. Our family is no exception, for we too have evolved our own version of how things must be done at Christmas time - acceptable perhaps only to us, but acceptable because grown from our own expression of family.

Some of the ideas that have been born and brought up with our family will never leave any of us, wherever we go. Others have been short-lived. They have been tried and immediately discarded. For instance, there was the year I had the splendid idea of placing a special lighted candle on the table for each member of our family not with us for Christmas. We started this custom, most enthusiastically, a few years ago when I lost my oldest daughter to a handsome American.[34]

I still had three daughters left and lots of Christmases ahead, I thought. And it was such a lovely idea, in keeping with the sentiment of the season. We all agreed it would be so touching to come to the Christmas table and remember, looking at this candle, the one who could not be with us, but whom we all remembered at this time with affection, tinged with a little sentimental regret. The others would know that when their time came to leave the family circle, their candles would also be placed on the table and they would be remembered.

Alas for such happy thoughts! Had I realized the difference one little year can make in a family of three grown daughters, I would have thought better than to institute the Candle Custom.

For, before I had properly recovered from the first departure, my second child married and moved away from our home. However, I still had two.

Or had, until recently.

The youngest has now decided to join her sister in the United States for a look at life away from home. The other, teaching in Labrador, views with dismay the picture that a Christmas at home now presents for her.

[34] Rhona, the oldest, married the American serviceman in 1957 and moved to the U.S. soon afterwards. The mass exodus had begun. The second child, I moved to Joe Batt's Arm (Fogo Island) in 1958 and married there three years later. In late 1962 Peggy, who had joined her sister in the U.S., was married in Massachusetts, followed within a few months by June, who found her husband in Northwest River, Labrador.

Her three sisters have gone. Her old friends have scattered, as old friends will. She has, with our wholehearted approval, elected to satisfy her curiosity about Christmas in Labrador.

So there we are! Shall we, my husband and I, together with our one remaining child, a small son of five years, march into our dining room, bearing four candles for our dear departed daughters happily enjoying their Christmas away from home? As if we could ever forget the full tables we have always had.

Thus it was that this particular bright idea died a sudden and well deserved death.

But there have been other, happier customs. Some of them my daughters will carry into the bosoms of their own families. Others were just for us, and have gone forever. Yet they remain with us all, keeping green the memory of "those wonderful Christmases at home, when we were young."

We never had a proper meal on Christmas Eve. I was always far too busy. Instead I spread a Christmas paper tablecloth on the floor of the living room. Everybody simply squat down on the floor and enjoyed hot dogs or hamburgers or sandwiches – anything one could pick up and eat. Nobody ever minded missing dinner. Not on Christmas Eve!

Of course, there had to be something special, even for an occasion instituted to save mother extra work! So I would probably bring out the first of the Christmas cakes and cookies, made well ahead of time.

With the advent of television, this proved increasingly popular and was extended to include the two meals of the day. It made so much less work than a full meal, and was always an exciting occasion. Nevertheless, as the girls grew older and washed more dishes, there was a back-to-the-table movement. However, the custom served its purpose for a period, which was all it was ever designed to do, and I recommend it for families with scads of small fry.

Another thing we did that was a little different was the giving of table gifts. These were not proper Christmas gifts, but just some little item to add to the festivity of the table. After the excitement of opening the usual gifts had subsided, it was always refreshing to have one more to look forward to!

This custom varied with the years. As the children grew into their teens, despising tin whistles, dolls' boots and bangles, I took to placing nylons and necklaces by the side of their plates.

But it was not always thus! Usually, I made a large firecracker, with the gifts tucked inside. Of course, they had to be small items, but it was novel and exciting for them, and made a really nice centrepiece besides. To make it I saved three empty soup cans, so that another ritual at our house was invariably tomato soup for lunch the day before Christmas Eve! Both ends had to be removed from the cans, which were laid in a long row, end to end. The gifts were wrapped and placed inside, with the tag bearing the recipient's name attached to the gift by a good long length of red twine, long enough to reach outside the firecracker, when made. As a final step, the cans were wrapped in red crepe paper, reaching out a few inches from the ends of the cans. The paper ends were twisted together and tied with bright bows. Then the big firecracker was placed in the centre of the table, the gaudy tags trailing along the white tablecloth, all ready to be yanked out by squealing youngsters.

Where on earth did I get this nice idea? Why, I read it, years ago, in *Chatelaine*.

There was one year when we made an extra special event of our table gifts. Each child, on going to the table, found a slip of paper containing a rhyme. The rhyme directed her, as humorously as possible, to where her gifts lay hidden, and dinner could not be served until each child had discovered where hers was.

It was an extremely popular game, but it did not last. For one thing, I ran out of rhymes. For another, it delayed dinner. Add to that the fact that the children soon outgrew the search anyway. But it was the best of fun while it lasted, and makes another of those happy little memories of Christmas that a family cherishes once it has broken up.

One of the oldest of our family customs is that there must be an innovation each Christmas. Around about November I begin to think "What on earth shall I do this year?" The new simply *must* go with the old, and strange to say, I have always found something a little different for each Christmas. Sometimes it has been a family project, like making decorations. One year we took to decorating the bedrooms. Another year we frosted all the windows with Christmas scenes. Never again! It took me days to get the windows back to normal.

Then there was the year we practiced carols and went around the neighbourhood, singing with great gusto – and in harmony! And the year we decided to visit the Orthopaedic Hospital and bring gifts and candy to the little ones. This was a successful and rewarding venture which we did several times after.

Some years I would make a change, perhaps, in our accepted pattern of decoration. Not the tree. That must never change, for none of us ever see prettier trees anywhere than in our home. It is, we have been told, the European method of decorating a tree, and that is probably so, for I first saw a tree done in this way by an English lady when I was quite small myself. My older sister copied it for our household, and ever since we have all of us carried it into our own families.

Ornaments may be used if desired, bells, balls and so forth, but they are not necessary. We use lights, plenty of them, and then we simply load the branches of the tree with silver icicles. Not just a miserable strand here and another there, but all that the branches will bear. We spend hours putting it on, and it must go on one strand at a time if you want to get the right effect. Our tree is a dazzling sight, with the lights shimmering through the icicles.

I don't know why, but we have always put a white sheet or two around the foot of the tree, lumping it up here and there unevenly. No one else that I know of does this, but we rather like it. It gives a finishing touch to the well-dressed tree. We lay our gifts around, on the sheet, and there is no sign of bare floor at all.

No, the tree never changes. But other things are permitted to change. Sometimes I do something different in the way of a dessert or trimmings. One year I made the hard sauce into little snowmen. Another year I made a house of gingerbread with windows and doors and an outdoor scene. It was rather crude, as I'm not much of a craftsman. Yet, when it was done, it managed to look too special to eat!

Last year we had a cookie tree for our small son, and any children who came to see our tree went away with a few of the cookies that were hung for decorations. It was just our way of using an unwanted tree top, but it looks now as if we shall have to find such a top for some year to come.

Like most families, we open nothing until Christmas morning, and of course, we must all be there for the event. The year my daughter had her firstborn, we fidgeted through a delay caused by her insistence on having her "Opening" ceremony at her home, so that her less-than-one-year-old should miss nothing, after which they obliged us by turning up for *our* "Opening" ceremony.

We all sit on the floor, and from now on, the show belongs to Daddy. He picks up each gift, reads the tag and passes it over to the one concerned. Then we all sit in a state of blessed excitement while the numerous gifts are distributed. Then we start ripping, tearing, exclaiming, squealing, kissing and oh-ohing. Everybody pitches in to clear up the Christmas litter and the morning settles away to appreciative sniffs of turkey dinner.

Church is a must in our family. Some attend the midnight service on Christmas Eve, others turn out for early service on Christmas morning. Indeed, one of our treasured family memories is to recall trudging homewards through the snows of other Christmases, with the dawn just beginning to break. There was always something special then about the world we walked through. Partly, it was the stillness, and the feeling that we were awake and aware of this glorious Christmas morning, while others still slept in their beds. Partly, it was – oh, a great many little things, I suppose, that, when you think of them all simply add up to the Christmas feeling.

In later years when the girls sang in the church choir and had to attend eleven o'clock matins, the Opening of the Gifts had to take place in between services, so that all of us could be on hand.

Even when, after the girls were grown and found themselves unexpectedly with an extremely late arrival in the form of a baby brother, we still managed to be together for the gift opening. We got around the child's problem, once he was old enough to enjoy his first taste of Christmas, by contenting him with his stocking until his sisters got back from church. Since the gifts under the tree were wrapped anyway, and since we were careful to include lots of small toys in his stocking, he had always been perfectly content to wait. To him, as to the rest of us, waiting for the others is all part of Christmas Day.

We always have our Christmas dinner at one o'clock. One of the best customs I have inaugurated is that the girls do the Christmas dinner dishes, while I have a nap. I need it. Truly, I do. Besides, I take over for the rest of the day.

For the evening meal we simply have sandwich snacks. I go all out preparing the sandwich plate. Refreshed by my nap, I am more than willing to spend a couple of hours "fixing." I couldn't go to more trouble for special company than I do for this occasion. I enjoy doing it, and I enjoy the appreciative remarks that greet my preparations.

Nobody ever wants to eat lunch on Boxing Day, and this is an occasion for simply raiding cookie jars and cake tins and the fridge. There's food on hand in plenty for anyone that wants to take the trouble to prepare it but Boxing Day is my holiday. For the evening meal, I bestir myself, and get out the salads and cold cuts, which I have prepared as far as possible in advance. We also have our special dessert on this occasion. It is made for Christmas Day but nobody ever eats it. That too, apparently, has become one of our hard and fast Christmas customs.

I always make plum pudding, but invariably, that is enjoyed whenever the time comes to make soup of the turkey bones. I can't recall any Christmas Day when anyone could find room for plum pudding, or any other dessert, after the rest of the dinner was eaten.

Following the diet of excessive meats and rich desserts, our family appetite turns to other fare, and the very day after Boxing Day finds us indulging with newly found appreciation in that much loved and well known Newfoundland meal, fish and brewis.

When the children were small, an outing "downtown" was, of course, part of the Christmas doings. We made a ball of it. We ate at a restaurant, looked at the toyshops, shopped if anything were needed, and maybe went to the Raffles.

I don't know how widespread the custom of "Christmas Raffles" is in other provinces, but we've always had them here in Newfoundland. Vacant shops on Water Street, our shopping centre in St. John's, are taken over by various charity concerns, mainly the orphanages. Christmas wouldn't seem like Christmas at all on Water Street if one could not hear the harsh, tinny bells calling all and sundry to "hurry, hurry, hurry" and win a giant turkey or something equally delectable. It wouldn't be complete without this, any more than it would without the melodious chimes of the church bells.

Snow generally comes to us just in time for Christmas. Occasionally, we have a green Christmas, and when we do, we don't like it. However, as long as you don't look outdoors, it isn't too bad, for with the glittering tree and the gaudy Christmas decorations, it is not difficult to pretend that the ground outside is white with snow.

Naturally, part of our Christmas activities includes touring the city to look at the lights. Some people go all out with the aspect of the season's preparations, and the result is always worth the grand tour. For our part, we have always been content with the lantern over the door and an outdoor tree hung with coloured lights. We just haven't gone in much for the outdoor effect.

Many of our neighbours have done much better than this, and it is a favourite pastime of ours to look out the window and admire the decorations, at the same time trying to figure out who is entertaining whom up the street this evening. But, as we turn our heads away and see our house glowing and glittering with the efforts and planning of days, even weeks, we feel we have everything.

Every single Christmas card received has found a resting place. Usually, they are strung on tinsel and looped around the top of the walls. Which reminds me of another little custom of mine. Usually, Christmas cards are delightfully gaudy, but always you will come across two or three that are truly beautiful. Maybe the colours appeal to you, maybe the scenery or the message. With me, it is usually a combination of scenery and colour.

Anyway, when I find "my" card, I pin this one up over the kitchen table, so that I can see a bit of beautiful Christmas in front of me as I make my preparations.

There was a time when Christmas meant a period of anxious planning. Now, everything seems to go forward smoothly and on schedule. Don't tell me the years have something to do with it. I know darn well they have!

The time I like best of all is late Christmas Eve. Everybody who is at home has gone to bed, and only I am left pottering around, always finding one more job to do, putting out nuts and candy, adjusting decorations, adding last minute Christmas cards to the garlanded tinsel, listening to Christmas music.

Another year, another Christmas. And here I am again, looking forward to another Christmas Eve, to that very special time for me, while I wait for the two o'clock entrance of those of the family who have gone to Midnight Service.

Only, this year there will be no entrance. The house will be warm with decorations, joyous with music, but quiet - oh, far too quiet!

And I - I am luckier than most. For I still have my small son, and Christmas will never be really lonely, ever.

THE STORY OF PETER (1963)

Rabbits are the cutest, cuddliest pets anyone could ever wish for. I can assure you of this from personal experience. A rabbit has everything a cat or a dog has as a pet, plus a decided advantage in that he can neither bark nor meow. He cannot whine. He cannot even undermine your resolution by looking at you pleadingly.

We had a rabbit. We had him for nearly two years. We brought him home with us from Joe Batt's Arm, a settlement on Fogo Island. People there, many of them, keep rabbits like other people keep cats, and the little creatures are to be seen scampering around the hills, free as the birds, and will come home to the barn at night.

Our rabbit was tiny when we took him away. He was a male, with just a touch of white on an otherwise black body. Naturally, we called him Peter. Before long, Peter was the pet of the whole neighbourhood. He would allow anybody to pick him up, would even run to people to have his long ears scratched.

I remember one time, showing off my dog to a small visitor. The dog, a friendly creature if ever there was one, came up and started to lick the child. The little boy began to cry, and I said, "Dear, the dog won't hurt you."

"Oh yes, he will," came the tearful reply. "He's tasting me now!"

Peter was like that. He was the lickin'est rabbit you ever saw. He would start at your fingertips and lick his way industriously up your arm. He only stopped licking if you would consent to rub or scratch him, when he would crouch as still as only a rabbit can.

Our little black rabbit was completely housebroken. That meant we could have him around the house whenever we wanted, which was often. Apart from an unfortunate tendency to chew books and lamp cords, his house manners were perfect. He would jump in my lap and cuddle up until I grew tired of him. After a few pleadings to be petted some more, he would give up, jump on the most comfortable chair in the room, or stretch out in front of the fire and enjoy the warmth.

Peter's tastes in food varied. Naturally, he was fond of the usual rabbit diet of green grass, lettuce, cabbage, carrots. But he learned to like other foods, and particularly relished a meal of baked beans, or macaroni and cheese, with a slice of bread and butter for dessert, all washed down with a dish of chocolate milk. He loved ice cream, candy, potato chips and cake. Best of all, he liked arrowroot biscuits. We always kept a package in the cupboard for him, which we offered from time to time as a reward for good behaviour.

Peter learned to rise on his hind legs, sniff, scratch and otherwise examine the handle of the cupboard door. I would then open it and pass the box of biscuits to him, as you would pass a box of chocolates to an adult. He would take one out of the box – just one, picking it up daintily in his long front teeth, very neatly, very politely, then scramble off to some favourite corner to nibble it.

At times, when nobody could be bothered with him and he wanted petting, Peter would settle down by our dog, Buttons, who was always ready to devote his spare time to licking the rabbit's ears. They got along fine together, although the dog was sometimes a little jealous. I have seen him many times gobbling up food that had been set out for Peter, and not because he liked it either. For what dog honestly enjoys eating raw carrot?

The first summer we had our rabbit, we fixed up a space in the back garden for him and fenced it about with chicken wire. Evening, I would bring him indoors, and he would have his hour with the family before retiring to his dwelling in the basement. He lived there during the worst of the winter weather.

But by the second summer, Peter had grown to be a big strong, male rabbit. We were afraid he would dig his way out of his pen, for he had the most intense dislike of it. But no. He would scratch holes, but never deep ones. We learned that only female rabbits dig burrows and hide away in them. Peter had a simpler method. He chewed holes through the chicken wire, and got out as often as his bunny heart could desire.

This posed problems, for he would turn up anywhere and everywhere. Fortunately, he was a well-known character in the neighbourhood. In fact, there were two or three families that he visited fairly regularly, looking for a change of diet. Someone would always pick him up and bring him home.

This sort of thing went on until the wire fence had been shifted in every possible way, its holes covered with pieces of wood, large rocks and more wire. But neither stone walls nor iron bars could deter Peter once he had decided to take a ramble around town. We gave up, finally, in despair. I opened the back door for him every morning (he was always right there beside it, waiting) and let him go. And every evening, I would see him loping in across the neighbouring gardens, heading for home and supper. The door was left open for him until he chose to come in.

The dogs around never tried to harm him. In fact, one day I saw Peter chasing a small dog. The game had started with the dog chasing Peter in wide circles around the garden. But Peter was so swift that in no time at all it was he who was chasing the dog. The canine population accepted Peter as one of themselves. Cats, I noticed, were not so friendly. They were extremely curious, and would sit around for hours, just staring with round eyes, sometimes even venturing up close. But they would not play with him.

Everything was fine and dandy. We had a rabbit so tame that he was housebroken, would answer to his name, presented no feeding problems and could be let run about. But Peter must often have wondered whether he was a dog or a rabbit. Maybe he was trying to settle the question the day he disappeared.

I was not seriously disturbed. Peter always came back. I hoped he wasn't in the same position as the dog I read about who had visited the supermarket. The loud-speaker in the store suddenly blared this desperate announcement: "Whoever lost the German shepherd, please come to the meat department right away."

Rabbits are excellent food, I'll admit, but Peter would have made a poor stew, although it was naturally a standing joke in the family that we'd never be stuck for a meal as long as Peter was around. As one who was extremely fond of rabbit meat, I have to admit that I have never since been able to enjoy it. I am reminded of lines written by Oscar Williams, in "Shopping for Meat in Winter":

What lewd, naked and revolting shape is this?
A frozen oxtail in the butcher's shop
Long and lifeless upon the huge block of wood
On which the ogre's axe begins chop chop.

The sun like incense fumes on the smoky glass,
The street frets with people, the winter wind
Thrown knives, prices dangle from shoppers' mouths
While the grim vegetables, on parade, bring to mind

The great countryside bathed in golden sleep,
The trees, the bees, the soft peace everywhere –
I think of the cow's tail, how all summer long
It beat the shapes of harps into the air.

Two days passed. Then I had a telephone call. It was from my doctor. He had been visiting in a neighbourhood quite distant from mine, and had been struck by the sight of a tame black rabbit in this house. Having seen our Peter before, he soon put two and two together. The good doctor, bless his rabbit-loving heart, brought our rabbit back to us, carefully deposited in a large carton, which in turn was sealed up with scads of adhesive tape.

Peter's adventure soon came to light. At this time, there had been some street repair work going on, and a night watchman had set up headquarters in a small temporary shelter. Always in a fever to investigate anything strange, Peter had of course gone exploring. The watchman, once he made sure he hadn't had one too many when he saw a black bunny rambling about a city street, picked it up. Having a kind heart, and not knowing what on earth else to do with his strange find, he brought it home, where our doctor had promptly recognized it.

So, for several weeks, all was well again. Then one day Peter disappeared once more. It was inevitable, I suppose. We have seen or heard nothing of him since. I advertised my loss, but the only call I received was from a woman offering to give me her two rabbits. She was looking for a good home for them, she told me. She lived in the downtown area, and had to keep them on the roof of a nearby mercantile building, which proves there is more overhead than telephone wires.

We have all missed our Peter very keenly, and while I don't think I shall ever again attempt to bring up a rabbit as a house pet, he has been a worthwhile experience in our lives. We loved him dearly.

I have wondered about him many times, whether he is safe and well or whether some dreadful accident befell him. I shall never know. But I truly hope that somewhere, in a little heaven reserved for bunny rabbits, Peter – like "Old Shep" – will have a good home.

LABRADOR WEDDING (1964)

Being city bred and a mother, I naturally took some care in choosing what I should wear at the wedding of my daughter, which was to take place at Northwest River, Labrador.

Northwest River, twenty miles from Goose airport, is a place of great natural beauty. The warmth of its hospitality and sincerity of its way of life give it immeasurable charm and dignity.

Bearing in mind the fact that I was going to the frozen north, I made only one concession to the approaching spring – a hat. My dress was a simple any-season affair of brown on beige. I chose pretty green shoes to match my hat and a necklace to match both. I felt confident, as I completed my packing, that I had not overdone things. I had not the slightest desire to appear stylish or to outshine the other mother at the wedding.

Yet, I readily persuaded myself to add just one little touch. After all, it was my daughter's wedding, and if I couldn't wear my new brown fur stole at my own daughter's wedding – well! Besides, it wasn't even real fur. I packed the stole. I also packed elbow length gloves and a dainty beige bag. And I packed my binoculars, a set of 7 x 50, which I wouldn't be caught dead without, and which was my wedding dress from the daughter before.

This, no doubt, needs explanation.

When the daughter before this one got married (I have too many daughters to bother explaining them all) my husband gave me the money to buy myself a new gown for the wedding.

Now, I already had a dress which was quite suitable for the occasion, although I saw no reason to explain this to my husband. It wasn't a brand new dress, true, but on that occasion such as this, I was travelling to a strange place for the wedding. I would be among people who had never seen this or any other of my dresses before. So what difference would it make?

Although I had a dress, I didn't have a set of binoculars, and I had wished for binoculars many, many times. My hobby of star-gazing has led me to the purchase of a telescope, but telescopes aren't particularly convenient to carry around and set up, whereas binoculars are handy to grab up at a moment's notice. So, I bought binoculars instead of a dress, and they have ever since been looked upon fondly in my family as "Mom's wedding dress."

There should have been ample opportunity for me to indulge my hobby, for rarely are the skies cloudy over Labrador. Yet I found myself so caught up with preparations for the wedding that my nocturnal activities seemed to consist of constant trips between somebody's house and the Community Hall where the reception was to be held.

Invariably, I took my binoculars on these expeditions. Invariably, too, I found myself over-burdened with such necessary nuptial requirements as thumbtacks, crepe paper, artificial roses, musilage, scissors, a large silver knife, several lengths in various widths of white ribbon, an assortment of snowy white linen tablecloths, and the centrepiece for the bridal table. My binoculars lay right at the bottom of my capacious handbag, as inaccessible as if I had left them on my dressing table.

I had therefore to pass up many an opportunity for star-gazing. Time was of the essence. Aunt Jane was waiting for the knife. She wanted to tie a white bow ribbon on it. Aunt Susan was expecting some help with frosting several dozen cakes. Aunt Liz was bound and determined that someone else was going to have to put up the decorations this time. And Mary, too young as yet to have earned the revered title of "aunt," was anxious to find someone to run over her solo with her.

To visit Labrador, however briefly, and come away without having seen the Northern Lights would indeed have been a sore disappointment to me. I was not disappointed. On this occasion, we had just left the hall, which we had been decorating for the event. And well I knew it! For hadn't I just been perching (a fearful, shivering bit of humanity, but a mother!) on a chair, the legs of which had been placed, two on one long bench, two on another? And hadn't I myself cut innumerable 4 by 12 inch strips of coloured crepe paper to hang around the big electric light fixtures?

It was not a cold night. In fact, I never did find it cold there. The early April sun warmed the day to an amazing degree, and I wished more than once as I trekked hither and yon, that I dared shed my Canadian kidskin jacket. The lack of winds tempered the climate to the point of downright comfort, so pleasant and enjoyable a contrast to the rain, drizzle and fog of the usual St. John's spring.

We were tracking, single file, over the snow. By now, I had been at Northwest River for three days, and I hadn't exactly been sitting on my behind all the time. Even visiting mothers are expected to pitch in and do their share, when the event is a wedding. Doing my share seemed to involve a great deal of plunging about through snow. The spring snow lacked firmness. It was beginning to soften and sink, a trap for the unsuspecting tenderfoot. I had by this time begun to develop an instinct for the true path which had come to me through repeated flounderings and sinkings into the much softer drifts that flanked the path.

Indeed, with experience, one learned to carry on a satisfactory three-way conversation while walking in single file, and I greatly admire, even if I could never acquire, the knack the livyers had of throwing the words back and forth through their teeth, so that they landed, like an aimed missile, right at the listener's ear. "The Lights are good tonight," came to me, whether from for'ard or stern, I couldn't say. Of course, I had already discovered that, and had missed my footing more than once because of it. They were better than good. They were most beautiful, far beyond anything I had ever seen of them before.

The Northern Lights can come in many ways. They can come as a ghost in the night, unrecognizable, flitting fancies of their true forms. You are looking at flimsy clouds or distant fog, you decide, and it is not until you notice you can still see the stars shining through the haze that you realize you are looking at an aurora.As you watch, spellbound, this diffuse illumination shifts and glows quietly. Usually, the lights are white, but often they show varying colours of yellows, reds and greens.

They can come, slithering and sliding silently across the sky, pushing out a coloured ray tentatively to the zenith, drawing it back again quickly. Other times they are in a feverish haste, darting back and forth, shooting out sharp fingers of light, or sending out streamers and beams that look like searchlights criss-crossing the sky.

They can come in great waves like an endlessly surging sea. Or they can come as I saw them, a vast glow of light that arched from east to west like a giant rainbow. Along its path shot out smaller arcs of light, spreading upwards and outwards, sharp like icicles, pointed like moon mountains.

Somewhere at the back of my mind had lurked the bizarre notion that the bridal group would have some means of transportation. If anyone had asked me outright if there were any motor cars in the village, I should have replied that I thought not. Nevertheless I should still have been absurdly confident that I, in my brown fur stole and pretty green shoes, would by some magical Labradorian process have been wafted over the unfriendly snows to the church.

I arrived at the church alright but only by trudging. Over my arm I carried a string shopping bag. In it were my green shoes, my beige gloves and bag. My stole lay over the white counterpane of my bed, back in the house. I could face the snows of Labrador in a spring hat, but not in a dress and stole! Arriving at the small church, which was filled to overflowing with Indians, Eskimos[35] and whites, we simply changed our shoes in the church porch. Later, we went through the same process at the Community Hall. I looked smugly at the decorations as we entered.

In a village where everybody is either an Aunt Sarah Jane or an Uncle Ben, a receiving line becomes an absurdity. So do a great many other formalities long cherished by larger societies.

The bridal table was handsome in white linen, lighted candles, and baskets of artificial sweetheart roses. The wedding cake could have taken its place with pride on any wedding board. Those nearest and dearest to the bride and groom took their places without benefit of place cards. Other people just "came" and at the far end of the hall, buffet tables had been set up to accommodate them.

The blessing was asked, refreshments were served, congratulatory messages were read, the wedding cake was cut. No speeches marred the conviviality of the occasion. The minister simply rose and wished the couple many years of happiness on behalf of us all.

Since anybody who wants to can go to a wedding, the gathering was large and somewhat mixed. While for the most part the people were white, there was also a goodly number of Indians and Eskimos. A wedding is no less an attraction to an Indian than to any other Labradorian. They simply crowded in through the door of the hall and stood there, staring their fill while we ate ours. I didn't think this at all unmannerly, considering that I

[35] "Indians" and "Eskimos" were contemporary terms for the Innu and Inuit.

myself had twisted my chair so as to be able to stare at them!

These were Montagnais Indians, and were a healthy looking lot, with their black eyes and hair startling against their coppery red skins. They live on the other side of the river and commute by means of a cable car, the only one in Newfoundland. Some of them, the boys particularly, were well dressed in the usual fur-trimmed parka. Others seemed simply to have fallen into whatever was nearest in the way of clothing, so that young children looked like women, and women looked like men.

The Eskimo has quickness of intellect and great pride. He is offended, and rightly so, if a tourist asks him to pose for a picture. He resents being thought of as an object of curiosity. The Indian, however, will pose gladly, with much giggling and gesturing.

It was on the night of the wedding that I had my first really good opportunity to look at the heavens. Everybody was energetically stomping out the measures of a Newfoundland Set, to the full-blooded rhythm of four lusty guitars. And where was I? Out staring at stars. I felt like Robert Frost in his poem "Come In":

> But no, I was out for stars;
> I would not come in.
> I meant not, even if asked,
> And I hadn't been.

Nobody missed me. Nobody would miss me. I was only the mother of the bride, no longer capable of rioting through the lengthy measures of the square dance.

In defence of my aging bones, I might say that in Labrador, as in other parts of Newfoundland, the success of a wedding is often judged by the length of time it is "kept up." While such a feat of endurance as this would impose on me was not altogether beyond me, I was, shall we say, ill-prepared to cope with it.

I had just stepped out for a breath of air, and also as an excuse to pass more closely by a group of chattering Indian youths. The heavens were a deep black. The stars looked as if they'd been splashed on by a careless painter. They scarcely twinkled, so still was the atmosphere.

I thought of my binoculars. My dainty beige bag had also been left lying on the white counterpane in my bedroom. I now carried a capacious travelling bag. Rummaging, I managed to extricate my binoculars which had become entangled with a corsage of pink mums. I had impatiently whisked off the corsage as a piece of superfluous finery.

I was delighted with the richness and variety thus offered me, for into my field of view leaped thousands of stars, clouds of stars. I hadn't felt so delighted since a Northern downy woodpecker entertained me in my garden a few weeks earlier.

Binoculars at a wedding? Why not? I warrant stranger things have been brought to weddings in mothers' handbags!

I left Northwest River regretfully, but feeling that I had crammed considerable experience into my short visit. I had ridden the snows in dog-team, snowmobile, and that marvel of transportation for the far north, the Ski-Doo.

I had entered the portals of a Hudson's Bay Trading Post. The thrill of doing so was not too greatly diminished by the startling realization that here was a modern, well-stocked supermarket. At the checkout I was served by an intelligent quick-gestured Eskimo.

I had crossed Northwest River in a cable car, along with a group of warmly parka'ed Indians.

I had ridden a Land Rover for twenty miles at what seemed an angle of 35 degrees, and was in a position to state authoritatively that these vehicles (if they are that, and not witches' broomsticks) can do all that and more than you have seen them perform on TV.

I had stood for two uneasy hours on the banks of Goose River, awaiting the taxi that was to take me to the airport, and realized for the first time the isolation of Northwest River. A great feeling of loneliness came upon me, and I wondered what would happen if our message had not got through and no taxi was on the way after all!

Some day, please God, I shall go back to this friendly and inviting land, shunned by an unaware and uncaring civilization. Its charms, strong and irresistible as they are inexplicable, will lure me back, as April lures the crocus from the snow. (That lovely phrase is not original. It belongs to our Newfoundland poet, Ned Pratt.)

Until then I shall cherish my memories: of bushy tails fanning the crisp air as a dog team dwindles to a lone black spot on the frozen wastes of Lake Melville; of the Mealy Mountains heaving out of the flatlands; of the Mission Chapel across the river in the Indian settlement; of this friendly little settlement; and of the still nights, the howl of the huskies, and the brilliance of the constellations against the deep black sky. Carl Sandberg says it so much better in "The People Yes":

> And the Labrador sunset shortens
> to a nocturne of clear stars
> Serene over the short spray
> of Northern Lights.

ALL ABOUT STARS (1959-69)

"All About Stars" drew the attention of the Royal Astronomical Society of Canada. Several of the columns were published in the RASC's National Newsletter. *Others found their way into* The Review of Popular Astronomy *("Sizing up the Supergiants" in 1960) and the* Ottawa Journal *("The Tearful Maidens" in 1961). Far removed from politics, Dora Russell was still venturing into the male-centred world around her with her columns, unique combinations of hard science and ancient mythology.*

This series proved exceptionally popular. Dora received many notes of appreciation from her readers. A few were critical, wondering when she was going to begin reading their horoscopes. She ignored such requests. But one reader kept insisting that he had received the first ever letter from outer space! This man, apparently deranged, was offended that Dora was ignoring him. Her response, finally, was to write "How to send mail through Outer Space," reprinted at the end of this section.

THE ASTRONAUTS

A new word has been added to the English language. It is a word that will crop up frequently in future talk of space travel. The word is "astronaut" and it means one who sails to the stars.

When Jason of ancient mythology sailed in search of the Golden Fleece, he called his ship the Argo and the men who sailed her were the Argonauts. The Southern Hemisphere contains the constellation Argo, complete with sail and oar and helm. Thus Jason's ship is commemorated in the skies.

The word "astronaut" is an excellent choice for the seven men who have been picked to be the first human space travellers. Their voyage will be every bit as perilous as Jason's, and the unknown quantities will be as numerous.

The United States has planned Project Mercury as the first attempt to put man into space. These star sailors will guide their space capsule around the earth at first and will probably do no more than decide when to slow the capsule down in order to descend. Even this much may at first be done by ground stations.

The true space ship will not come until later, and it will probably travel to the moon and back. This time the crew will be in full control and will make all the decisions, important and otherwise. Some people wonder why a space ship cannot be guided at first by automatic pilots. Airplanes fly many millions of miles each year with the help of automatic pilots, yet no one doubts for a minute the need for human pilots. It will be the same in space.

The astronauts, all seven of them, were very carefully picked. All sorts of factors were taken into account: physical fitness, mental fitness, mechanical and other abilities, courage, intelligence, and the ability to make decisions. All have undergone the most severe tests that American ingenuity could devise. By the time their voyage becomes a reality, they will have been thoroughly trained in every respect for the hazards they will have to face. Everything that can be foreseen will have been dealt with. It is the unknown quantity that cannot be planned in advance, and it is here that the only real danger lies.

A common first reaction on learning that men are ready and willing to venture into space is amazement. How can they?

How can they indeed! It is easy enough to liken their project to the first sailors of the sea and the first fliers in the air. Yet this is different. These men will leave the dust of the earth, not to sail its waters or to fly its atmosphere, but to vanish into what is still a great unknown. On their return, our thoughts about space will never be the same again. We will come to accept space travel as part of our way of life.

THE RINGS OF SATURN

One of the showpieces of the heavens is Saturn, the planet that is surrounded by a beautiful and quite unique system of rings. There is nothing like them in the entire heavens. Seen in a telescope, the spectacle is remarkable in the extreme. A breathtakingly lovely ring, thin and disconnected but perfect in shape, floats around the gigantic sphere. Although Saturn is far from being as bright as Jupiter, its rings make the most magnificent object that human eye could ever behold.

Galileo was the first to see the now famous rings, and he surely must have been startled almost out of his very considerable wits. At first it looked as if the planet had some odd sort of appendages attached to it. Then it began to look to him like a triple system of stars. He never did find out what the strange sight was that he had encountered while looking through the world's first telescope.

Later, with more powerful telescopes, the rings were seen to better advantage. It was thought that Saturn was surrounded by stationary gold arches, but the laws of mechanics subsequently disproved this. Besides as time went on and telescopic work began to develop a little, it was soon observed that the rings were rotating. In fact, the outer rings were rotating more quickly than the inner ones, and this difference in velocity alone would be enough to break up a solid arch.

Then, for a time, it was thought that the rings might be in a liquid state, but this theory was soon refuted by the fact that there would, in such a case, be waves raised by the tidal forces of the planet which must eventually lead to disruption.

The conclusion was finally reached that the rings are immense swarms of tiny particles circling the planet, each body a very wee moon.

As to how this strange and unique state of affairs came to be, there are two possible answers. One is that the rings are material that were supposed to form a satellite but never got around to doing so. The other supposition is the one which is widely accepted: the rings are the remains of a satellite that came too close to the planet and paid the penalty. There is a limit of safety, known as Roche's Line, beyond which it is madness for a satellite to go. This one-time moon came too close to the giant planet, and was consequently torn to pieces by the tidal forces of Saturn.

It is probable that Saturn never did miss the moon it lost, since it had a pretty good stock of satellites anyway. As if the beauty of the planet and its rings were not enough, Saturn is an impressive sight also by reason of its many moons, for outside the planet's rings are no less than nine satellites.

One of those moons, larger than ours, is distinctive because it is the only satellite believed to have an atmosphere!

THE SCORPION

Ever tempted to let your son drive your car?

Never, never do it! For, if Greek legend has anything to do with it, disaster must result.

Once upon a time, Apollo, the sun god, allowed his dearly beloved son Phaeton, to drive the horses of the sun's chariot on its daily journey from the eastern to the western horizon. But the big, bad scorpion appeared and frightened the horses, so that poor Phaeton was dashed to the earth.

Another legend connects the Scorpion with Orion, the hunter. The Scorpion is supposed to have sprung out of the earth at Juno's command. Juno had been rather irritated at the conceit of Orion who, it must be admitted, rather fancied himself the dashing hero. Juno ordered the Scorpion to attack Orion. He did so, and caused his death.

Both Orion and Scorpius were eventually placed in the heavens, but whoever did the placing could surely have ranked as today's greatest diplomat. The two constellations were so arranged that they never, never appear together. Just as Orion sinks in the west, the Scorpion raises his wary head in the east.

Originally, the constellation of Scorpius extended much farther than it does today. When the ancients decided to mark off a constellation for every month of the year (the zodiac) they found themselves with twelve months, but only eleven constellations. So they amputated Scorpius, making a separate constellation of his claws which now form another constellation, Libra.

Most constellations require a fertile imagination on the part of the viewer to see in them the shape they are supposed to represent. Not so, Scorpius. It is a beautiful group, very easily traced, and its bright stars are formed in such a way as actually to suggest a scorpion.

It lies just under Ophiuchus and between Sagittarius and Libra. Maybe you know none of these constellations. In that case, try looking for the Heart of the Scorpion, a first magnitude star named Antares.

Antares is not too difficult to locate for the simple reason that it is the only really bright star in the southern part of the sky. Then again, it has an unmistakable reddish hue. If you can find Antares, you may be able to trace the rest of the constellation, or most of it. It looks exactly like a fishhook. Near Antares you will find a row of three nice looking stars. These are the Scorpion's head and claws - rather short claws, as I have already explained. The tail which contains a pair of stars is called the Cat's Eyes.

I have looked in vain to see this constellation in its entirety, and have come to the reluctant conclusion that it is located too far south to see at all. However, we do have Antares and a portion of the Scorpion. Remember, when looking for Antares, that there is a planet very near that might confuse you. Antares is distinctly red. The brilliant Jupiter is very yellow, very bright and very "planetish."

THE NOBLE LION

In the days of ancient Egypt when summer was at its height, the lions would come sniffing and prowling in from the dry desert lands to gulp the welcome waters of the Nile.

The time of the Lions was also the time of the Sun, for in those days, the sun entered the sign of Leo a month before it is due there today. All Egypt watched and waited then for the great rising of the waters. They made the constellation of Leo the Lion sacred to Osiris. Perhaps that is why so many Egyptian pillars and monuments are adorned with the likeness of the lion.

In mythology, however, the lion stands in the skies for the first labour of Hercules, the slaying of a fearsome lion that had come from the moon to terrorize the inhabitants of earth. The lion was eventually borne back to the skies, but so was his killer, the hero Hercules. As to who keeps an eye on which, mythology remains silent.

Some people believe that the Sphinx represents Virgo's head on Leo's body.

To come down to modern times, Leo is still high in the southern horizon these nights, although he is beginning to lower his shaggy mane to the west. It is a striking and beautiful constellation. Most people know the part of the Lion that forms his head. Called the Sickle, it looks like a great question mark in the sky. I think I knew those stars before I knew the Dipper, because they made such a remarkable group in the early summer evenings.

To find Leo, turn your back on Cassiopeia and the Dipper, facing south. High in the sky before you is Leo, the Lion. It is a large constellation, the most conspicuous of the Zodiac constellations, most of which are rather colourless.

Or, use the two stars of the Dipper next to the handle - the back stars. Follow a line southward through these stars. You will first hit the star forming the shoulder of the lion, then you come to Regulus. The sickle that forms the lion's head is clear and unmistakable, and at the bottom of the sickle's handle gleams the bright star, the heart of the lion, Regulus of first magnitude. The rest of the constellation forms a triangle of three stars, marking the animal's rear end, and here we have a fine second magnitude star right in the tip of his tail. This is Denebola. The sickle shape and the triangular tail are easy to identify. Denebola is of interest because it forms, with Arcturus, Cor Caroli and Spica, the Virgin's Diamond.

One other star of interest in the constellation is Gamma Leonis. Near the lower part of the sickle, it is a lovely double star, golden orange in colour, a contrast to the intense white of Regulus and the orange of nearby Arcturus.

DAY OF THE SHORTEST SHADOW

The Chinese had a very uncomplicated method of determining when one season was over and another began. They simply measured the length of the shadows. The day on which the shortest shadow was cast at noon was the first day of summer, and the longest shadow at noon was thrown on the day that winter began. We call it the summer and winter solstice.

On June 21 the sun is at its most northern point, shining high overhead. It takes the northern half of the earth longer to turn through the sunny day than through the night; therefore nights are short and days are long.

The summer solstice is the first day of summer for the north, but it is winter in the south. After June 21-22 you will see the sun going a tiny bit more to the south each day, until it finally reaches the equator. That is on September 23 when autumn begins, and when day and night are of equal length again.

It is the inclination of the earth's axis that brings us dreary winter and bright summer. If that axis happened to be perpendicular to the earth's orbit, instead of being inclined as it is to an angle of 23 degrees, there would be no seasons. Then we could all pick ourselves a nice hot spot, and go there to live with the assurance that it would stay hot. It would have its advantages! However, the axis of the earth is tilted, and we do have changes of season as a result. But, if (to use proper terms) the ecliptic were on a plane with the equator, there would be no different seasons.

If that axis were one day to be inclined at a greater angle than it is at the present, there would be much more pronounced differences in the seasons than we experience today.

As a matter of proven fact, the climates on earth were vastly different in ages past. Tremendous upheavals that have taken place all over the globe seem definitely to have been caused by some astronomical catastrophe that completely changed the sun's radiation on the earth.

A shift in the position of earth's axis could cause such climatic changes and terrific upheavals to which the earth's surface still bears witness. According to one writer, it was this shifting of the axis that caused the sun to stand still for Joshua.

There is, I suppose, no way of proving that the earth at one time received a very violent blow, say from a collision with another celestial body. Nevertheless, there have been these violent upheavals more than once in earth's span of life, powerful enough to change the face of the globe and to cause incredible changes in climate. The shifting of the axis could do this.

Then again, it is difficult to conceive of anything that could possibly cause the axis to shift unless it were some powerful body from outer space that collided or nearly collided with the earth.

THE JULY SKIES

It gives me great pleasure, ladies and gentlemen, to introduce the stars of summer, and with them to express the hope that we get more clear skies this season than we did during the so-called spring.

Sometimes it's so long between one clear night and another that a constellation disappears before you have time to wave goodbye to it. Leo is so far into the west now that unless you are very familiar with its stars you would not trace its outline. Virgo is visible only in the early part of the evening.

The summer stars are quite lovely. There's a softness and warmth to them. A figment of the imagination, no doubt, but a pleasant one. There are some splendid constellations hung in the galleries of heaven these nights. The southern part of the sky is especially pretty. The Scorpion crawls across the sky, followed closely by the Archer with its teapot shape. Scorpius has the bright star

Antares to give it added beauty, and the twinkling redness of this star confirms its name, which means "rival of Mars." In addition there are the two planets Jupiter and Saturn which appear in these constellations. The southern sky is full of interest.

Above Scorpius we have the figure of Ophiuchus, the serpent holder, and on each side of him, divided into two parts, is the Serpent. Directly over the head of Ophiuchus is Hercules.

The Big Dipper has by now veered round to the northwest with the handle uppermost. Following its curve, we come to Boötes and then to Virgo. Cassiopeia is now in the northwest, right side up, with Cepheus above her. The Little Dipper runs up from Polaris and the Dragon winds around it just below Hercules.

Lyra is high in the east with its brilliant star Verga, and directly below this is the Northern Cross, loveliest of the summer show. Below and to the right of this we have Aquila the Eagle.

Planet positions for the month are as follows: Venus is brilliant as an evening star in the west, appearing in Leo the Lion. She will remain there until the middle of August after which she will disappear from view, appearing later in Leo as a morning star. Mars is also in Leo, very close to Venus, and as a result very faint for a planet. Jupiter is visible most of the night appearing just outside Scorpius. Actually it is in the constellation of Libra. Saturn, not nearly as bright as Jupiter but holding its own among the stars, is also visible most of the night and may be found in Sagittarius. Both Saturn and Jupiter appear first over the Southside Hills. Mercury may be seen after July 8, appearing low in the western sky after sunset.

As for meteoric showers, Cygnus the Swan is the best radiant point this month. On July 4 there should be a swift shower appearing near it. Another will emanate from the direction of Deneb in Cygnus near July 19. Towards the end of the month there will be one in Aquarius but that will be quite late at night.

KING CEPHEUS

"Cepheus illumes the neighboring heavens, still faithful to his queen."

Cassiopeia, Queen of Ethiopia, had a husband. His name was Cepheus (pronounced see-fuhs). He plays the part of the jealous husband, watching over his beautiful but vain spouse. Their daughter Andromeda and her lover Perseus are near also, but that is another story.

Some say that the honour of a place in the sky was given Cepheus because of his contribution to the part that he played in the famous expedition of the Argonauts in quest of the Golden Fleece.

The old star atlases picture him seated on his throne in state, with his scepter in his left hand and his right hand holding his royal robes. Quite an imposing picture. More practical people, however, see a much simpler figure - a triangle on top of a rude square. He is rather a dim constellation, not nearly so bright and beautiful as his wife, but then, that is as it should be.

To find him, face north. Like Cassiopeia, he has only five stars, looking somewhat like the picture of a house with a peaked room drawn by a small child. Some people see him as a large K open to Cassiopeia. He lies partly in the Milky Way between Cassiopeia and the Dragon, but closer to the pole than to Cassiopeia. He is almost in line with the Dipper, but on the opposite side of the pole.

An imaginary line drawn from the pointers of the Dipper and extended about five times its length will lead you to the pole star. If you extend that line, you will strike a star called Gamma Cephei. That's the King's cap.

This star, along with two others, the brightest and the second brightest (alpha and beta), are of extreme interest because in the course of time they will become the pole star. So, in 4500, 6000 and 7500 years' time, Cepheus will be a very important constellation indeed.

One of the stars in Cepheus is a supergiant. It is a very faint star to look at. Nevertheless it has a diameter a thousand times bigger than that of the sun. In other words, if this giant of a star could be placed where the sun is now, it would extend beyond the orbit of Jupiter, with the result that Venus, Earth and Mars would be completely swallowed up. How's that for size?

Gamma, the top star in his head, is the radiant point of a display of meteors, the Cepheids, which are seen each year towards the end of June. In days gone by, the appearance of the Cepheids was hailed as a storm warning.

"Oft shalt thou see, ere brooding storms arise,
Star after star glide headlong down the skies."[36]

PERSEUS AND ANDROMEDA

Sometimes the gods of old put whole families in the sky willy-nilly, as was the case with the group of constellations known as the Royal Family.

[36] Virgil, *The Georgics*, Book I.

Of those constellations concerned, Cepheus and Cassiopeia are circumpolar and may be seen any night of the year. Perseus is now below Cassiopeia, rising in the northeast. Cetus is in the southeast, preceded by the Great Square which contains the Winged Horse.

The huge animal has his back toward the horizon, his feet in the air. What he hopes to accomplish by galloping feet up is more than I can venture to say. However, since the fair lady Andromeda whom he intends to carry off is standing on her head nearby, one must merely conclude that they did things differently in those far-off days.

According to Greek legend, Andromeda was the lovely daughter of Cepheus, King of Ethiopia, and his queen Cassiopeia.

Cassiopeia was as vain as she was beautiful, and audacious enough to insist that she was "the fairest of them all." Back in those days, such statements were not tolerated. The gods showed their displeasure by sending a sea monster (Cetus) to ravage the coasts of the kingdom.

Cepheus and Cassiopeia were at their wits' end, and begged for mercy. They were coldly informed by the gods that their country could be saved only through the sacrifice of their daughter Andromeda. She was to be chained to a great rock by the sea, where she must await her fate at the jaws of the beast.

Meantime back on the range, our hero Perseus had been busy cleaving off the horrible head of Medusa, the Gorgon, which turned to stone all who beheld it. Naturally Perseus, being a fastidious soul, wouldn't look anyway.

Chancing upon the fair Andromeda, Perseus assessed the situation at a glance, whipped out the Gorgon's head and turned the monster to stone. Then he bore the fair maiden away as his bride, on his famous steed, Pegasus, the Winged Horse. (Heroes in those days had everything to work with!)

Charles Kingsley, in *Heroes*, tells it all beautifully.

> *And when they died, the ancients say, Athene took them up into the sky, with Cepheus and Cassiopeia. And there on starlight nights you may see them shining still: Cepheus with his kingly crown, and Cassiopeia in her ivory chair, plaiting her star-spangled tresses, and Perseus with the Gorgon's head, and fair Andromeda beside him, spreading her long white arms across the heaven, as she stood when chained to the stone for the monster. All night long they shine, for a beacon to wandering sailors; but all day they feast with the gods, on the still blue peaks of Olympus.*

THE LADY IN THE CHAIR

Next to Orion and the Big Dipper, Cassiopeia is the most widely known constellation. No doubt this is mainly because, being a circumpolar constellation, it does not rise and set as the others do. It goes round and round continually and can therefore be seen on any night of the year. It is conspicuous, too, because of its striking shape which is quite unmistakable. It is a zig-zag row of five stars that form an almost regular W or M in the sky, depending on its position at the time.

When one looks at Cassiopeia, one is apt to see only those five stars, but the constellation is quite rich in stars containing no fewer than one hundred. It is enough for one night to find and admire its clearly marked outline. The second night you look at it, as your eyes become accustomed to seeking out the white spots on a dark background and as your neck becomes comfortably stiff, you will see many fainter stars in and around the outline. If you have field glasses or a telescope, you can spend nights on this one constellation alone, seeking out the double stars and the patches of nebulous material.

Cassiopeia lies in the path of the Milky Way, which is why it is so rich in stellar matter. To locate it, lift your eyes to the usual starting point, the Big Dipper. Find the star where the bowl and the handle meet and sight a line from this, on through the Pole Star, and you come to Cassiopeia. It is situated at the same distance from the Pole Star as is the Bear, but on the opposite side of it.

In fact, during the course of the night, Cassiopeia and the Big Dipper circle the heavens like the opposite sides of a great wheel. Around 9 o'clock on a May night (if the fog lifts) you will see the Dipper hanging upside down and Cassiopeia standing right side up opposite it. As the earth turns, Cassiopeia climbs into the northeastern sky while the Dipper drops down below to the northwest.

Cassiopeia is a lady and the W is a chair. Hence "the lady in the chair." She is the Queen of Ethiopia but is different in legend from most of the other constellations. Usually a place in the sky is reserved only for heroes or ladies in distress, or given as a reward for great service. But not so with our lady Cassiopeia. She was put in the heavens by the gods as punishment for her extreme vanity in declaring that she was the "fairest of them all." And if you do not consider the punishment a severe one, how would you like to sit upside down in a chair for six months of the year?

It's an ill wind, however, that blows nobody any good. Cassiopeia's loss is our gain, for she makes the finest illuminated clock that one could have for free. With a little practice in observing the changes in position of her five stars with reference to the pole, you can readily tell the time at night.

COLORADO, HERE I COME

Robert Frost must surely have had Newfoundland in mind when he wrote these lines (from "Two Tramps in Mud Time"):

The sun was warm but the wind was chill.
You know how it is with an April day
When the sun is out and the wind is still.
You're one month on in the middle of May.
But if you so much as dare to speak,
A cloud comes over the sunlit arch,
A wind comes off a frozen peak,
And you're two months back in the middle of March.

March, April, May. Mine not to reason why spring weather never comes in the spring season, for I am off to a place where "I may sit and rightly spell of every star that heaven doth show."[37]

Newfoundland is a good place to come back to. It's also a good place to get away from, and there's no better season than the spring to leave its dear old soil.

[37] John Milton, "Il Penseroso."

So, come Easter time, I shall, with considerable joy, put away the snowsuits and mittens, buy a ton or two of mothballs, and hang up the skates and the slides. No more winter for me! I shall lovingly press all the summer clothes, even those which I am not taking with me, and I shall leave instructions for someone else to do the spring cleaning! Of course, I realize I may have to wear my winter coat to the airport, but someone can bring it back home again for me.

As you read this, I shall probably have reached my destination in the state of Colorado. My daughter and her little family live at Colorado Springs. Once the usual tears of reunion have been properly shed, I shall go out to see my other friends, the stars.

For many years I have wished, in rather a vague way, not dreaming that it would ever become possible, that I could visit an observatory. The thought of actually looking through a giant telescope is enough to "send me up a wall," as my offspring would put it. Maybe I shall have my wish, maybe not.

Denver City, which is only "around the Bay" from Colorado Springs, has a very good observatory. I had hoped to make a couple of trips down there to see "the stars in silence shine" but this may not be possible. However there is an amateur Astronomical Society and also a Planetarium in the Springs. I think the Air Force has one there. So I am bound to have something new to tell about.

Please don't think however, that because I am gone, my column will go too. I shall leave a good supply of articles behind me, and if I find something very special to tell about out there, I shall send some back.

The skies will look a little different there, and it will be interesting to compare what I see with what I have left in Newfoundland. Denver is in the same latitude as Washington, 40 degrees, and Gander is 49, so there will not be very much difference. However, I am hoping to see few of the more southern stars that almost, but not quite, show themselves in our latitudes. And, of course, I shall have a much better opportunity to see the comet than you people will, for the Colorado skies are among the clearest that one could wish to see.

So, "prepare my starry nights," and let not one of them be clouds, for Colorado, here I come!

COLORADO SKIES

Wouldn't you think that stars would look the same, no matter in what part of the world you lived? It isn't so. Naturally, whatever half of the sky one sees at any particular point on earth is not the same as it is in some quite different latitude. Naturally, southern skies are completely different from northern skies. There are different stars and constellations to be seen in each hemisphere. That is not what I mean.

Here in Colorado, the stars themselves look different. They look bigger, brighter, delicately coloured. They appear in large numbers right down to the very rim of the horizon, so that you feel if you could only ride out to the horizon, you could easily reach out and pluck one from the skies. Even our winter stars at home cannot match the summer skies of Colorado.

We are ten degrees more southerly latitude here than in Newfoundland, so that I see 10 degrees more of the southern skies.

When I first came here, in April, Orion was still visible, and I saw that he was higher in the sky than at home, as were also the nearby constellations of Canis Major and Minor, Taurus, Gemini, and the rest of the splendid winter show.

Underneath the feet of Orion is the small constellation of Lepus, the Hare, which we see at home only on the clearer nights. It is plainly visible here, and underneath again, is Columba, the Dove, which we do not see at all at home. Part of the large group of stars forming the southern constellation of Centaurus is invisible here, as is also Corona Australis, the Southern Crown, which lies just underneath Sagittarius. Eridanus, which represents the River Po and which streams outward from the feet of Orion, can be seen in full in its proper season.

I think the first thing that drew my attention when I looked at the skies here was the constellation of Coma Berenice's (Berenice's Hair). This small group is really an open cluster, like the Pleiades. Some twenty or thirty stars can be seen with an opera glass. If you like facts on a larger scale, how about this: in this small constellation it is estimated that over 100 nebulae are located in a space no greater than that which is covered by a full moon.

Coma Berenice, visible as a faint hazy patch on a clear moonless night, lies near the curve of the Big Dipper's handle. If you know where to find it, the group is distinguishable at home when the Dipper is high in the sky, as it is at this time of year. But it never seems to stand out clearly, or ever look anything like the pictures one sees of it.

So, the very first thing that caught my eye when I looked at the Colorado skies was this little constellation, standing out so clearly, and so unmistakable in shape that the difference in its appearance here, and at home, was truly amazing.

The Aurora Borealis, or Northern Lights, are very seldom seen here, and never do they put on such a fine display as they give us in Newfoundland.

We do not run on Daylight Savings Time here, so that we see the planet Jupiter rising early, about ten o'clock, and its brilliance completely outshines nearby Saturn. Both are to be found in the constellation of Sagittarius.

THE BASEBALL DIAMOND

By the time this appears in print, this year's World Series will be added to the history of baseball. But echoes of the highlights of the series will be in the air for a while yet. My money is on the Dodgers, and I hope they will have a nice baseball diamond reserved for them in the sky, where they can play ball forever.

There is indeed, a section of the sky that resembles a baseball diamond. The gods of mythology would probably place me in the sky as a warning to humanity for this, but, thank goodness, they don't know how to read!

Shades of Pegasus! For it is the Winged Horse itself, or part of it anyway, that I am likening to a baseball diamond!

The Great Square of Pegasus is high enough in the eastern sky now for good viewing. Once you have found it, you will never forget it. The eye is certainly taken by this large square formed by four bright stars. Besides the Square, there are other stars that form the constellation of Andromeda and Pegasus itself. The Square, of course, is the baseball diamond, and it is not at all difficult, when you look at it, to find home plate, first, second and third bases, and even the right and left field foul lines.

This Great Square, one of the stellar landmarks, is important to know. For one thing, Andromeda extends from it. Andromeda is important because it contains the one and only visible spiral nebula. A spiral nebula is a Milky Way system like our own, and when you see this particular one, you see what our galaxy looks like. Of course you need a telescope, but the object is visible to the naked eye as a fuzzy star.

The Square has always been important to mariners, particularly when the northern sky was clouded. Knowing this Square was the means of saving the lives of Donald MacMillan and his companions when they were lost in the Arctic. So you see, a knowledge of the stars is not so impractical as it may seem.

If you can't find the Great Square of Pegasus simply by looking around the eastern sky, try a more precise method. A line drawn from the Pole Star through the outside star of Cassiopeia (that will be the west end) leads to two bright stars which form one side of the square. This line hits the eastern side of this rather imperfect square, each of whose sides are about fifteen degrees in length. (Remember the pointers of the Big Dipper are five degrees apart. This is a great help in measuring a rough distance with the eye.)

Another way to find it is to continue a line drawn from Vega through the centre of the Northern Cross. This will also point to the Square.

All four of these corner stars are rushing towards us at inconceivable speeds. One of them, the north eastern one, is the head of Andromeda. Another, called Scheat, is of an absolutely enormous size. Astronomers tell us that if Scheat were placed where the sun is, the whole of the orbit of Venus would be engulfed by it!

When you have found the Square, test your eyesight by counting the stars within it. At first glance, it seems there aren't any, so bright are the corner stars. But you will soon begin to see a good many of them. Thirty can be counted with ease, and some people claim to having counted a hundred, on a good clear moonless night. Naturally, the telescope shows many more. Hundreds more. Thousands more. Some of these are pretty double stars, and some of them are grouped in beautiful clusters.

HOW TO SEND MAIL THROUGH OUTER SPACE

Sir:

Your correspondent Jack Robertson has referred to me as being an authority on space, and complains because I gave him the brush-off when he phoned to tell me he had received a letter from space.

I wish to apologize for my impatience, but the fact of the matter is that I was rather taken aback, perhaps a little piqued, having expected myself to have been the recipient of the first mail from space. After all, I am the authority, not Mr. Robertson. I am also an authority on many other things, including the proper use of instant mashed potatoes.

Having disposed of these preliminary comments, I shall now proceed to give Mr. Robertson some advice on the receipt and dispatch of space mail. I must warn him first to proceed cautiously in the identification of such letters, as there are many earth people quite capable of perpetrating a hoax on unsuspecting persons.

I therefore draw the following points to Mr. Robertson's attention:

The letter must be burned to a crisp. Travelling through the Van Allen radiation belts would consume all letters, including the mailbags. I've no doubt, Mr. Robertson, that this is why your postmark was illegible.

In addition to being consumed, the letter should, if it has come a long way, be perforated from the impact of micro-meteors. Even so small an object as a letter would not escape this bombardment of meteoric dust.

Newton's Third Law of Motion states that for every action there is an equal and opposite reaction. Determine the reaction, and see if it is equal and/or opposite.

If you wish to ascertain whether this letter comes from some point within the Solar System or whether it comes from beyond, you must first determine whether the letter has travelled faster than light. If it hasn't, then it has come from Venus or Mars or one of the moons of Jupiter. If it has, then it has come from some remote island universe probably in the vicinity of Cygnus or possibly Virgo. Determine how many billions of years the letter has been en route and you will then know how far it has travelled.

A letter coming from the vast regions of outer space will, of course, follow the contours of space itself, eventually closing in on itself. I'm not an authority on this, I am quite willing to admit. My source is Mr. Einstein who assured me most earnestly that space does indeed turn around and close in on itself. This has an interesting effect on space mail, since it means you don't have to lick the flap. The envelope will turn on itself and seal itself.

I have thought the whole thing out carefully, and have arrived at the following conclusion: A letter setting out through space at the rate of 186,000 miles per second would describe a great cosmic circle and return to its source after a little more than 200 billion terrestrial years.

If, therefore, Mr. Robertson's reply to this letter he claims to have received from space miscarries due to insufficient postage or illegible writing, his letter will be returned to him about 200 billion years from now. This is a rather long wait.

Mr. Robertson has been signally honoured by receiving the first letter from space. I don't wish to be personal, Mr. Editor, but why did they pick him instead of me?

Here is my conclusion. Gravitation, again according to my friend Mr. Einstein, is simply a part of inertia. It is my considered opinion that these beings from outer space selected Mr. Robertson because they have been attracted by his inertia. Furthermore, these beings from outer space have very little intelligence anyway!

Yours very truly,
Dora Russell
January 31, 1961

PART III: PERSONAL WRITING REMINISCENCES

In 1978, I asked Dora to write for me her recollections of her early life, especially the years she spent as a magistrate's wife in Springdale, Harbour Breton and Woody Point, Bonne Bay. I was at the time working on a biography of my father - The Life & Times of Ted Russell, *later revised as* Uncle Mose: The Life of Ted Russell *- and needed the guidance of her perspective. I am now sharing selected excerpts from those private writings to readers of this book, as they provide additional insight into Dora Russell, the woman.*

SPRINGDALE (1935-39)

With the news in 1935 of Ted's appointment as magistrate, we decided to have our much delayed honeymoon on Little Bay Islands. It was a beautiful place.

Two weeks later we set up house in Springdale where we were to spend the next four years. How did I feel about moving outside the city? I couldn't wait! To live in an outport, to be high on the social scale, which meant to me that there would be things I could do for the community. I had no regrets leaving St. John's but I was mighty homesick during much of my stay in Springdale.

Nothing is ever as you dream it must be. Neither was Springdale. It was then a place of about 900 people. Having been bred in the city, I found outport living rather difficult and was young enough to be very unsure as to what part a magistrate's wife was expected to play. Eventually, I found it amounted to merely being president of this or of that.

The religion was United Church. We went to church, although one Sunday after a two weeks' absence I was horrified to have to walk through a spider's web to reach our appointed pew. Sometimes I played the organ when the regular was not available.

Dancing was not tolerated, nor card playing. One had to draw the blinds if playing cards. Later, when I was better established, a handful of us women decided to use a barn and I was to teach them to waltz and foxtrot. Jen and Maggie Warr were among the avid enthusiasts. We had fun, but only for a while, for we learned that we were not to have the barn.

At first I had a toleration of Springdale, afterwards a liking of sorts. I had some good friends there, but it was often dreadfully lonely when Ted had to go away for a week or two. It was at this time that I began to read the host of classics that he had brought with him, and they filled many an empty hour. He had a trunkful. For the first time I became acquainted with Lord Lytton, Charles Reade, Stevenson, Kingsley - and of many works that I might never have read but for those lonely times in Springdale.

Once our furniture was paid for, Ted bought me a piano. I would open the front door and play, hoping someone might enjoy it or want to come in and hear me. Some hope!

The community was beautiful, then. Now it is a hodge-podge - too many houses for too little land. The people, despite their stern religious principles, were extremely kind to me, bringing gifts of cooked dishes, food, etc. when Ted was away. But for a new bride, life at first was disheartening. It was *too* cold. I cried when I had to clean frozen herring. I could not make friends easily – not at first. But eventually I took to the life and was proud to invite my city friends and family to visit me.

Hall's Bay was so peacefully beautiful. There was cod-jigging and sometimes a motor boat run. There was hole-in-the-ice fishing in the early spring. There was glorious salmon fishing. My best memory – to rise at three o'clock a.m. and walk the three miles to Indian River. The flies were so bad that we wore a netting over our heads. I caught three salmon, one of which must have taken me over an hour as it sulked under a log. (I never did much trouting, nor ever cared much for it.) In the early dawn the birds would flit across my path (I often went salmon fishing alone) and one could hear the growling of bears in the nearby hills. I was always very nervous when hefting home my catch of salmon, as often bears would follow the fisherman with his salmon sling over his back. The man would drop a salmon if pressed, and give himself time to go at a faster pace while the bear was devouring the salmon. I am happy, as I was then, to say that no bear ever followed me. How brave I must have been in those days, and me a city girl!

Ted was instrumental in forming a branch of the Jubilee Guilds (now a branch of the Women's Institute of Canada and still flourishing). We used an old store that stood across the road from our house (no longer there). There was a small corner room which served Ted as an office. We held our monthly meetings and often got together by day to learn to card and spin wool and to weave. I wove a blanket. It shrank when I was forced to wash it but did duty in the crib for years. In later years, back in St. John's, I served on the executive committee of the Jubilee Guilds.

We had two children born to us while in Springdale. In each case I had to come to St. John's for the birth. I couldn't stand the looks of the midwife, who had permanently dirty fingernails and three layers of grimy petticoats underlaying a rusty-black long dress.

Our first, Rhona, was born October 27, 1936. I came home for the birth, Ted joined me later and we went back to Springdale together. Ted was quite impressed with his first-born - couldn't stop looking at her. "One of these days," he said, "when she is grown, I shall tell her how clean you kept her." He never did, of course, but the point is that a daily morning bath and a nightly wash was cleanliness beyond his experience.

My second child, Betty, was born in 1939, on February 26. Again I went home for the birth. This time it was not so easy. It necessitated a long dog-team run to Badger. We brought Rhona along – Ted accompanied us as far as Badger. This is one of my most cherished memories. There is nothing to equal a dog-team journey when you are blessed with good weather. Our driver had a team named after different brands of margarine. There was Solo, Good Luck, and other long-forgotten ones. Lead dogs, invariably bitches, were usually called "Lady."

On one of those journeys, on the way back from St. John's after Betty's arrival, we had to spend overnight in a tilt. We arranged to take turns tending the fire during the night but our driver ended up doing most of the tending. I lacked the necessary fortitude and although willing to do my share, I actually took over for only two short one-hour periods. I meant to do better but was too weary. I can't remember if we ate, or what we ate, on that trip. We must have done so. The main thing was to keep the fire going. Certainly the dogs ate. Their herring at day's end was a noisy and snarly event. I wasn't afraid of them, as they were tied up. Had they not been, I should have been terrified.

The work of the house grew harder as the children came along. For me, it was like pioneer work. The standard of housekeeping was high and one had to live up to it if one was to maintain the respect of others.

By the time we heard we were to be transferred to Harbour Breton, I found it a wrench to leave Springdale and its people. Of all the places we had to live in, I think Springdale remains in my mind as the educator to outport life, and perhaps the most important period of my life as a magistrate's wife.

HARBOUR BRETON (1939-40)

We moved to Harbour Breton in 1939, to stay for one year only. During that year, I came to life. I dearly loved the old Newman house that we lived in, with its wine cellar where I stored my jams, pickles and vegetables. It was a huge house, almost 100 feet long. There were three pantries, one after the other, a smallish (welcome change) kitchen, since the pantries took away much of the kitchen equipment, leaving the kitchen as more comfortable and enjoyable living quarters. There was a dumb waiter to the dining room which we used as a living room. The intended living room was bare. There was a large bedroom upstairs which I used for hanging laundry and the kids used for playing. We entertained the hospital staff and they us, so we had a good social life.

I did some war work there, knitted and learned to turn a heel. During the war we used to listen to our radio for the sound of Big Ben.As long as it sounded, we knew we were still alright. British children were being evacuated and we "put in" for four, as we had a large house. However, the refugee children found quarters in less isolated places.

Harbour Breton was far removed from Springdale in its style of living. We were free of the silly taboos that characterized the Springdale of those years. It was good to organize a concert, to plan dances, etc. It was here that I learned the square dances and was always eager to "stand up" to one. On one occasion, a fellow danced with me, but immediately on hearing I was the Magistrate's wife, he dropped out."I can't dance with the *Magistrate's* wife," he said. But he did. I made him do so.

Over the hills we found lovely ponds to fish in, and places for picnics. One time we reached a lovely waterfall. It was a hot day so I peeled off my clothes and took a "shower." Afterwards Ted and I went off into the woods! A few days later, we learned that someone else had been in that vicinity and had had the pleasure of seeing the Magistrate's wife in the nude. We didn't lose any popularity because of this, as we would have in Springdale.

The view of Harbour Breton Bay from our house was breathtaking. Majestic is the word. But I didn't care for the climate. The sea in bad weather would look rough and dark. One had to pass it to go through the village. Also we got severe ice storms when doors would be difficult to open and the path downhill too slippery to venture over.

We were not in Harbour Breton long enough for me to get any roots down. I liked the place very much, though, and could have become attached to it were it not for another transfer.

WOODY POINT, BONNE BAY (1940-43)

My introduction to Bonne Bay was bleak. We arrived on the *Northern Ranger* in early December of 1940. Snow drifts were piled so high that it was impossible for us to get into our house, which stood on a hill overlooking the bay. We drew our water by bucket from a stream on the property and had to hack through the ice to get at it.

Our daughter Betty was very ill with pneumonia, caught on board the boat due to running from over-hot saloon to over-cold deck. It took a long while to nurse her back to health. I held her in my arms days on end, with little relief. It was a cruel time of year to move a family with small children.

The beauty of the scene did not register with me until the following summer. The grounds were very beautiful. We had a mass of poplars, which still stand; an R.C. church, which still stands; and some flowers I planted (still growing wild when I last visited the place in 1976). Blueberries were plentiful. The house we occupied was the former priest's residence. It had a chemical toilet – a bit better than the outdoor toilet in Springdale.

Things improved with time. I made many friends. I got a choir going. We made our caps and gowns and got to sing in harmony. I loved it. I also recall knitting endless pairs of full-length stockings for the children. Ted used to help with the Monday wash. We had to heat the water, boil clothes in lye water, starch, etc. One wash, two rinses – in an old-fashioned tub. The wash itself took from nine o'clock to three o'clock to complete as in Woody Point our two children increased to four. June and Peggy were born while we were there: June on the kitchen table with a very capable midwife in attendance and Peggy at the cottage hospital in Norris Point.

I especially remember riding on horse and sleigh on the Bay. The sleighs were the "side-on" type and the horses had bells. We had a good life there.

We spent over three years there but eventually we had to uproot yet again. Ted was appointed director of co-operatives with the Commission of Government, so back we went to St. John's.

DIARY ST. JOHN'S (1943-50)

Dora kept a regular diary intermittently from December 4, 1942 to March 18, 1950. It is not a daily diary; for most months there are six or seven entries, and occasionally a month or so will pass by with no entries. There is a significant gap from late 1945 through mid-1948, roughly the period of her employment at The Evening Telegram. *A secondary diary also exists in which she records accounts of various family related trips she took during the 1960s. These diaries, along with "Reminiscences," are currently in the possession of Russell family members.*

December 4, 1942

This is to be a diary to settle disputes, so we'll begin by establishing one fact - that this is the first real day of winter. Snow we've had - come and gone - but today we have a real blizzard and plenty of snow.

Well, here we are, with Rhona at 6, Betty nearly 4, June 17 months and Peggy 6 months. June is adorable - is just walking but talks plenty and has done so for some time. Rhona is doing fine in school. Of Betty there's no record to make. She's just Betty.

December 16, 1942

A catastrophe broke last Saturday night, December 12, when the new Knights of Columbus Hostel built by Canadians for the recreation of their service men caught fire. About a hundred people perished, over 30 of whom were Canadian service men. A mass funeral was held yesterday afternoon. The civilian loss of life was great too, but nothing very definite has yet been published. It was a ghastly affair, from the stories we've heard of it.

January 19, 1943

Day of days this. One to be remembered without pleasure, but definitely with awe at our incredible luck. Our kitchen pipe runs up through the roof and today about noon, as I *happened* to enter our bedroom (over kitchen) I saw that the ceiling around the pipe was in flames. Ted *happened* to be home and between us we put it out with very little trouble. Ted got a ladder whilst I got a bucket of water. It looked desperate for a moment when the bucket wouldn't go up through the damn hole in the ceiling and Ted lost most of it over me but saved enough to check the fire. I brought a pail the next time and it went up OK. Then we got Selby Parsons in to take the pipes down and fit them into the chimney. The rest of the day was an orgy of soot and cleaning up.

February 7, 1943

Germans are practically routed out of Stalingrad now. Battle of Stalingrad was won several days ago. Germans are just about encircled in the Caucasus.

August 7, 1943

Heard from Ted last night. He has, naturally, accepted the post [director of co-operatives] and says we will live with Dad until something turns up. I'm sure by Ted's letter that he's right up in the air over this and I have to admit I'm mighty pleased myself. The city has too many advantages to scorn.

March 14, 1944

I'd just about given up the idea of keeping this wretched thing going, but I suppose an entry once a month wouldn't hurt any.

Had my 32nd birthday.

Peggy has been walking for quite some time. The children have had colds all month. Right now Rhona is just well enough to go to school and Betty and the babies are under the weather.

Started writing while Ted was away and did a series of articles which I brought down to the editor of *The Daily News*. Too political for women's reading, was the verdict. Try something along the Dorothy Dix line, was the request. So I complied, as best I could, and Mr. Currie[38] says they'll do, but he's to ring me when he has time so here am I expecting his call every darn day.

We have a chance of a house in Topsail belonging to Ken Drownes. Not final yet, but a good chance. Guess my hopes of summering in Bonne Bay are gone. Don't know why it is that I'm so feverish (there's no other word) to get back to Bonne Bay, except that to me now it spells peace and quiet and contentment, with the children gone for hours at a time. It seems to me that even if I did have the children on my hands there as now, I could recover my strength in spite of it.

June 1, 1944

Last Thursday our servant girl came unexpectedly. We'd sent to St. Anthony Orphanage for one and were told one would be coming but we didn't expect her along so soon. However, we manage with Mildred

[38] John Currie was owner and publisher of *The Daily News*.

(Stevens) sleeping in June's bed, June in mine and Ted on the day-bed. Meantime it gives me a little more freedom, although she's pretty, pretty green. However, she's a nice girl. Fifteen. They provided her with clothes and made darn good provision. She's quite healthy and clean. I gave her a perm and bought a spring coat from Effie, and she looks real smart now, I really have hopes of her. Although I think she will be slow to accept responsibility. She's pretty lonely and homesick. The first night I took her out for a walk, the next we went to a show. Saturday we went window shopping, Sunday another walk, Monday she stayed in and moped, Tuesday we saw a play at Canon Wood Hall – she enjoyed that.

July 17, 1944

The address is Topsail now. At this date, we are practically settled away. Our stairs are not bannistered, no painting done, and we haven't our pump, sink or toilet, and no cupboards or shelves.

Monday June 19 was one of the wettest, windiest days in history. We came in on June 20. House wasn't nearly ready but we made a go of it and were only too darned glad to do so.

Things have improved wonderfully. Everybody in the pink of health and temper. We've been around a bit. We've spent two afternoons with the kids at the Flats and picnicked under Topsail Hill. We've also been to the Octagon a few times – three, in fact.

August 22, 1944

The summer has been a very poor one. Very cold

and foggy all July and part of August. Last week - 13-20 - was our summer.

Nevertheless it's been a grand, carefree summer. I've put on some weight and am feeling fitter than I've ever felt - quite, quite happy. All that's lacking is some work of a congenial nature.

December 11, 1944

Rhona and Betty went out to town with Mildred to see "Snow White and the Seven Dwarfs." Ted and I also saw it, and joined a party at the house afterwards to go to the Old Colony Club.

Sent a batch of articles to *The Evening Telegram* and had a letter today accepting them. I hope.

Children are preparing for their Xmas concert. Both have several parts. Betty's goes:

If I were ten years old, or somewhere near
I'd speak a great long piece for you to hear.
But now, you see, I am so very small,
I only came to say 'I love you' that's all.

December 31, 1944

My articles have been appearing under the pen-name Portia. $2.50 per.

May 22, 1948

Ted has been busying himself in the garden, seeding the back. He brought home a number of pines, also an ash, an elm and an oak, from the government.

I continue to receive words of appreciation of my speech.

Political situation is tense. One more issue of the Confederate to write for, then freedom again! Pretty soon I shan't know what to be doing with myself.

May 23, 1948

Wrote a story this a.m. that had been running through my mind last night in bed. "The Foghorn" might do for *Atlantic Guardian*.

May 28, 1948

Spoke over VOCM for Confederation.

June 9, 1948

The first Referendum is over. Interest was intense that day, June 3rd. Ted and I went out early in the a.m. to vote at St. Pat's Auditorium. I came on home, plunged into spring cleaning, taking Mary out to vote in the afternoon. Dropped into Hdqters but very quiet. Many tales abroad of skullduggery. R.C. nuns turned out to vote.

Result of Referendum pleased neither RG nor Conf. In fact, it was a distinct shock to both. Looks like it will have to be a religious campaign from now on. A lot of bigwigs coming in with us.

Ted left this morning for Fogo district, ostensibly to visit his Co-ops but he intends to get in a little informal politics.

Was on the air Tuesday before Referendum June 1. This time an interview with Mrs. George Brown. Also wrote a speech same day for Greg Power to read.[39]

[39] Gregory Power (1909-1997) was Smallwood's right-hand man during the struggle for Confederation. Later, Power endowed the Gregory J. Power Award, an annual competition at Memorial University to encourage young poets. He was also an accomplished athlete.

Ted and I sat up with a bottle to hear the Returns. Felt pretty low next couple of days, had expected Conf to top the ballot. Ted got quite drunk Friday evening.

June 24, 1948

Ted and I went down to Confederate Hdqters this afternoon. Joe wants me to write some more so I suppose I must dig in again for a while.

June 26, 1948

Wrote for the Confed this morning, then made June's and Ted's birthday cake.

July 6, 1948

Political doings started up yesterday, with a Confederate rally in the CLB Armoury and a broadcast by Bradley. We had a Co-op Council meeting and only got the last few minutes of the political meeting, then went home to hear Bradley. It's Crosbie tomorrow night.[40]

July 19, 1948

The most notable thing since last entry has been the consistently bad weather, often necessitating the lighting of the furnace. We've had three fine days lately but not hot. Ted has almost finished painting the fence, helped valiantly by Rhona.

We went out one night to see how the RG rally was getting along, then went down to Headquarters.

[40] Chesley Crosbie, a St. John's businessman, was a delegate to the National Convention. He supported responsible government, though for a time was leader of a group advocating economic union with the United States. His colleague in that venture was Don Jamieson, who would go on to have a successful career in broadcasting as well as in federal politics.

Downtown with Rhona this afternoon to get her a hat. My, Bowrings is certainly something to look at! I've opened an account there.

Spent 2-3 days on a job for *Atlantic Guardian* writing up a picture story. Don't know whether I'll get paid for it or not, probably not.

Some talk of my going over to Bell Island to speak on political platform. It was a report from Ted but I dare say Joe put the kibosh on it.

July 25, 1948

Things are gloomily quiet around town these days, but we Confederates are happy enough. 5000 majority so far. Rhona and Betty stayed up the night of July 22 to 1 a.m. taking down the count. I got a great thrill when we gained our first majority.

Had some encouraging mail from *Star Weekly* and *Colliers*. They would be interested in an article about Smallwood.

It begins to look like a general election in the spring. A delegation to Ottawa is the next step, appointed by the Governor. It is inconceivable that, even though we do not have a great majority, we should be forced to accept responsible government.

August 6, 1948

Since last writing I've had a few days' holiday. Went into the shack with Ted, leaving Monday and coming home today. Ted had poor weather but I had it fine all the way through for three glorious days. The first day we had some fishing at Country Pond and I caught three trout. The second day we picked strawberries at the

Nuddick. The third we tramped to Barney's Pond, right up to the head. I hoped to see beavers but was disappointed in that. We took a lunch and enjoyed several "spells." The view was magnificent, with ponds stretching in every direction.

We decided to have a young Canadian and did what we could about it.

I had word from *Star Weekly* and *Colliers* that they would be interested in a Confederation article. I tried something for *Colliers* and sent it off, but missed Ted's help and really don't expect results. However, in interviewing Smallwood he gave me an idea for a book – "Newfoundland, the New Province." Ted thinks well of it and will help me. Intend to buckle down to it right away but am now engaged in doing a second job for *Atlantic Guardian*.

November 24, 1948

Finished my article on how to do two jobs at once.

November 27, 1948

Finished article I've had on the go for some time. I've called it "Two Careers." Sent my book chapters off to Longmans, Green and "Day by Day" scripts to a couple of syndicated concerns. Don't feel too hopeful about any of it.

January 7, 1949

I was thrilled over the governor's new year address, in which he read an old article of mine – "Give us Men" (March 1946).

Got "The New Province" returned from Longmans. Too specialized, they said. No market for such a book.

Guess I'll just give it up or try to turn some of it into articles.

January 14, 1949

Thurs night I attended a meeting of the Home and School Association, and it was pretty ghastly. I ought to stick to it, or try to, but I must confess, the idea does not comfort me. Mr. Quinn presided and he was a slow and halting talker who spoke as if he were teaching and cast frequent glances at the blackboard behind him as if he were going to write down the answers as we spoke. I went through the school [Macpherson Academy] and it's very nice indeed. Saw the kids' rooms, recognizing them by the plants they had brought the day before. Meanwhile Ted went to the debate, where I had wanted to go. Joe lost his debate on the affirmative of "Resolved that the terms [of union] are adequate."

January 15, 1949

I plan to settle down next week and see if I can get some real writing done. I have been out a lot this week and with that and getting the kids' clothes fixed up I haven't had a minute. However, except for some sewing I am fairly well ahead with things now, enough to see some spare time looming up.

I forgot to mention our having seen "Henry V" (Shakespeare) with Laurence Olivier. We took Rhona and we all enjoyed it tremendously.

January 18, 1949

Peggy Lou seems to have a variety of boyfriends. She brought a new one home with her today – Robert. It seems she's all washed up with Charlie. The beautiful friendship began in this way. Peg: "Will you be my boyfriend?" Boy: "The one who I throws snow at, I'll be her boyfriend." "And," reported Peg delightedly, "He frew snow at *me*." But if snow was the start, it was also the end, as next day Peg came home disgusted. "I'm not gonna have him for my boyfriend any more," she declared. "He frew snowballs at me today."

June also told a tale today. They were discussing Peg's teacher, whom Peg dearly loves. June insists she has freckles but Peg won't hear of her beloved teacher having freckles. She says it must be some other teacher that June sees.

February 17, 1949

Sent off article to *Colliers*. It's a good article but probably too late with it anyway.

June and Bet playing school. Both are teachers. Girls leave room and stay. Betty sends someone after them. Ditto June, "Mary, you go." Bet sends yet another, "Jean, go." Ditto June, "Jack, you go." "Oh," says a horrified Betty, "you can't send a boy into a girl's toilet." "Oh," says June, "Jack, come back here."

March 11, 1949

No go with *Colliers* or anything else, for that matter. I guess the trouble is that I can't write after all! At any rate, I certainly can't sell.

March 28, 1949

Announcement made today appointing A.J. Walsh as our Lt-Gov. That's a smack for Joe – he's been making public the fact that Outerbridge (Sir Leonard) would be Lt-Gov. and that he would be asked to form an interim cabinet. Since he's been proved wrong on one point maybe he'll be wrong on the other. His face is red today!

April 1, 1949

A Date!

Union at long last consummated. Ceremony was broadcast 1:30.

Kids trying to book orders for kittens.

Walsh got his appointment, a fact which hit Ted rather hard. He'd banked on the Man of Integrity not to assume office on the understanding that he would have to name Smallwood as provisional premier. Anyway, 'tis done. We moaned about it all day, then got over it sensibly.

April 9, 1949

All the kids of the neighbourhood are trooping in today to see the new babies. Pusstopher Catlumbus has her first brood of four and the kids are canvassing the neighbourhood taking orders.

Am nourishing the hope that I'll get a chance to enter politics. Have talked to Smallwood. Don't suppose there's much chance however for a poor ole woman.

April 28, 1949

The Liberal Convention starts tonight. Trains came in this morning, bringing delegates by the hundred. There will be 600-700. I'm a delegate for St. John's East.

A lot of water has passed under the bridge since April 9th, my last entry. Ted came home one morning, announcing that he had resigned his job and had decided on politics as a career. He had been down to see Joe, and had bargained for a cabinet post. It was a curious coincidence that I'd been down that very morning to see him too, wanting a district. I had a good chance of getting Fogo, but Joe decided that two in a family was too much. I might not have got it anyway. Joe was afraid that women in politics was too revolutionary, so after a couple of weeks hoping and planning, I settled down in resignation.

Ted is going for Bonavista South and feels very confident of winning the district. It's all very interesting these days. Drew, PC national leader, was here and made speeches but didn't seem to make an impression at all.

May 2, 1949

Ted said more to make a Liberal of me than anyone has yet said. But he didn't make a Liberal of me for all that. I don't think anyone ever will. Liberalism is only the next best thing as far as I'm concerned.

Ted left today by train with 30-40 delegates from Bonavista. He left chock full of beans. How anyone can turn *him* down is a mystery to me.

The kittens, which are adorable altogether and which will soon be leaving us, are getting along splendidly and are a source of constant delight and amusement. The children seem particularly delighted by the fact that they seem to the kittens to be giants.

There are political broadcasts most nights but I don't usually get to hear them. Quite a few co-op meetings lately. They seem to conflict. Anyway, I don't seem to have much interest as I don't expect to vote. We have for candidates in St John's East, Geoff Carnell and Jim Fagan.

May 16, 1949

Letter from Ted today. He appears to be plugging ahead slowly and steadily and is quietly confident although realizing his difficulties in Bonavista South. June burst into tears after I'd read the letter aloud. We all went into the den and traced his "odyssey" as he called it, on the map.

Had an interesting p.m. with Eamon Park, who is on the executive of the CCF party. I contacted him after hearing his radio broadcast and he came in for chat.

Attended a PC rally. Drew back again. Good meeting. Coldwell will be here Friday.

May 20, 1949

Went out to airport to meet CCF Coldwell and got my picture in *The Evening Telegram*.

Big rally last night - Paul Martin. Wonderful gathering. Place jammed.

June 4, 1949

Of course the big news is the election results. White Bay is not in yet and Labrader has yet to be held. Apart from these, the Liberals carried off 20 seats, Peter Cashin won Ferryland as an Independent, and the PCs got the other five. They got St. John's East, Hr. Main-Bell Island and Placentia. Ted took Bonavista South with a 2,000 majority. I was there for the final campaign. Went out on Wednesday night's train (May 25), got there dinner time. Had an afternoon meeting with the ladies and spoke 45 minutes.

About 200 women there. Spoke again at night meeting with Ted and Gordon Bradley. Got splendid reception, cheers, etc. It was wonderful. We both came back next day, Friday, which was election day, leaving at five in the afternoon and arriving home 2 a.m. I was sick almost all day but managed to hear the counts starting to roll in. Sunday there was no news and it was Monday before we got Ted's count. The children stayed home for a holiday to hear the count. They were awfully excited and I allowed each of them a new dress from the catalogue to celebrate.

June 6, 1949

Getting ahead with the gardening. Put in some seeds today and fixed up flower beds in back. Some nasturtiums in with the tulips under the wall, also larkspur. In a round bed I've put sweet peas, calendula, carnations and bachelor buttons. The children have theirs in too. I now have only the flowers in the front to tend to. We have half a dozen new flowering shrubs and the hedge seedlings are in.

June 26, 1949

St. Laurent[41] had a bumper meeting in Bannerman Park. He's a great man indeed. I wish he were CCF.

June 29, 1949

Terrific sweep for Liberal Party. Ted and I voted CCF but Gillies only picked up 175 votes. St John's East and West both put in Tories.

[41] Louis St. Laurent was the Liberal Prime Minister of Canada from 1948-57.

January 9, 1950

The children trooped back unwillingly to school today, after the Christmas vacation. The snow, which had held off (it was a green Xmas and New Year), came last night. It was very cold. The children did get in a bit of skating during the holidays but mostly the ponds were in dangerous condition.

Xmas was very pleasant. Ted stayed home Xmas Eve. Freeman and Clarence dropped in to persuade him to make the round with them but for once he remained firm. We were up early in the morning. Rhona got her watch, Betty a coaster, June $5 towards her bike and Peg her doll house and furniture. They all had new dresses and I had bought myself a midnight blue cocktail dress as a gift from Ted. All lace. Ted is quite taken with it. Our table gifts this year were from Ottawa – Ted had bought them. Mine was Chanel 5, which Rhona promptly dissipated by leaving it uncorked.

New Year's Day I had 13 visitors – Hons. Hefferton, Keough, Curtis, Drover with a couple of friends, Ken Carter, Captain Windsor, Dad, Joe, Powell and O'Neill.[42] Ted stayed home nursing a cold. He'd meant to take a week's holidays but the work piled up unexpectedly.

March 18, 1950

Ted bought his car today.

[42] Hefferton, Keough and Curtis were provincial cabinet ministers. The others on Dora's list, with the exception of Dad (my grandfather) and Joe (Smallwood), were personal friends and/or neighbours.

POSTSCRIPT

A NOTE ABOUT THE TEXT

Dora Russell was a pack-rat. After her death, the task of "sorting out the stuff" fell to me as executrix of her estate. With the help of family members, I recovered several scrapbooks and hard-cover notebooks in which she had pasted hundreds of individual newspaper columns as well as about a dozen manuscripts she had tried to have published over the years. (Unfortunately, most of the columns are undated.) I decided to combine this material with an equally abundant cache of papers belonging to my father who had died eight years earlier, and to donate the material to the Archives at Memorial University. That's where the Ted and Dora Russell Collection now resides.

Most of the text reproduced for this book was transcribed from that collection. There are notable exceptions. Before her death, Dora had decided to give her scrapbook of "All About Stars" columns (about 250 of them) to Randy Dodge, at that time president of the St. John's Chapter of the Royal Astronomical Society of Canada. Also not included in the Collection are Dora's more personal items: a scrapbook, several pages of reminiscences and her private diaries (held by family members). I do, however, transcribe excerpts from these papers in this book.

ACKNOWLEDGEMENTS

Many individuals helped make this book possible. I give full credit to Bert Riggs, archivist at Memorial University, for giving me the necessary nudge. He, along with staff members at the Archives and the Centre for Newfoundland Studies, assisted me as I gathered and sorted through a considerable batch of primary material, including well over 1,500 newspaper columns.

Then came the formidable task of transcribing. Unfortunately, most of the material has not been digitized (with the notable exception of the "Woman of the Week" columns transcribed by Elizabeth Browne, a librarian at Memorial University). I was, however, able to find many willing hands to help work through hundreds of original newspaper articles, many of which are showing their age! Invaluable assistance in this endeavour was provided by Wanda Stansbury and Peggy Vachon.

Thanks to Tonya Kearley, I also lucked into a group of students at St. Michael's Regional High School (Bell Island) who took on transcribing several of the articles as an assignment for one of their courses. My gratitude to the teacher (Melissa Deer) and the following students: Alicia Barnes, Tanner Bennett, Allison Boone, Samantha Carroll, Bobby Doyle, Rebecca Keels, Stephen Lahey, Keisha Noseworthy, Krista Taplin, Bradley Ubdergrove and Cameron Warren.

I appreciate the interest and professionalism shown by Donna Francis and her colleagues at Creative Book Publishing. I was most fortunate in having Joan Sullivan assigned to me as editor. We made a great team!

Special thanks to the following: Randy Dodge, for lending me his scrapbook; my siblings, who helped unearth long-forgotten photos; my friends Michael and Annette, for their hospitality; and my son Dennis, who nursed me through many attacks of "computeritis."

Elizabeth Miller

Daughter of Ted and Dora Russell, Dr. Elizabeth Miller spent all of her working life in the field of education. From 1958-68, she served as a high school teacher and principal in Joe Batt's Arm on Fogo Island. She left Joe Batt's Arm with her husband George Miller in 1968. After two years spent as Director of Communications with the Newfoundland Teachers' Association, in 1970 she joined the faculty (Department of English) of Memorial University. At MUN, Elizabeth taught courses at both undergraduate and graduate levels for the next thirty-two years. She received three significant awards: the Dean of Graduate Studies Award for Thesis Excellence (1988); the President's Award for Distinguished Teaching (1992); and the designation "Emeritus" (2004).

Elizabeth found her scholarly niche first of all in the field of Newfoundland Literature. She published two biographies (of Norman Duncan and Ted Russell) and edited several anthologies of short stories and poetry. In the early 1990s her research interests took a new direction: the novel Dracula (1897), its author (Bram Stoker) and its influence. Elizabeth is recognized internationally as one of the leading scholars. Even though she retired in 2002, she continues to make productive contributions through her publications, participates in radio/television documentaries and lectures at international venues.

Her research shows no signs of abating. Indeed, Elizabeth has re-embraced Newfoundland Studies with the publication of a collection of her mother's writing.

Elizabeth currently lives in Toronto. Her main non-academic interests include travel and baseball.